THE PEOPLE OF THE FAITH

THE
PEOPLE
OF THE
FAITH

The Story Behind the Church
of the Middle Ages

ANTHONY E. GILLES

Nihil Obstat:	Rev. Lawrence Landini, O.F.M.
	Rev. John J. Jennings
Imprimi Potest:	Rev. Jeremy Harrington, O.F.M.
	Provincial
Imprimatur:	+ James H. Garland, V.G.
	Archdiocese of Cincinnati
	July 3, 1986

The *nihil obstat* and *imprimatur* are a declaration that a book or pamphlet is considered to be free from doctrinal or moral error. It is not implied that those who have granted the *nihil obstat* and *imprimatur* agree with the contents, opinions or statements expressed.

Book design and cover by Julie Lonneman.

SBN 0-86716-067-5

TO BROTHER JOHN GORE, O.C.S.O.

THE PEOPLE OF GOD—FROM ABRAHAM TO US

A sweeping history of Judeo-Christian thought by Anthony E. Gillis.

Volumes available:

The People of the Book: The Story Behind the Old Testament. SBN 268 $5.95

The People of the Way: The Story Behind the New Testament. SBN 365 $5.95

The People of the Creed: The Story Behind the Early Church. SBN 462 $5.95

The People of the Faith: The Story Behind the Church of the Middle Ages. SBN 765 $6.95

Volumes in preparation:

The People of Anguish: The Story Behind the Reformation

The People of Hope: The Story Behind the Modern Church

PREFACE

Among Christians there have traditionally been two general reactions to medieval history. One is to view the Middle Ages as little more than a staging area for the Reformation. Proponents of this school of thought point to the abuses and contradictions within the medieval Church and say something along the lines of, "This is where the Church went wrong and why the Reformation was necessary." Advocates for this point of view look upon the Middle Ages as one great sin needing to be confessed, repented of and forgotten — as if the Middle Ages were a large tumor needing to be cut out of the body of history and thrown away.

The problem with this perspective is that it denies the essential interconnection between past and present. People who repudiate who they were yesterday will likewise disown who they are today. We cannot put the Middle Ages behind us as if they are no longer there; in reality they are forever stored away in our collective unconscious, influencing our thoughts and actions as much as the fifth or sixth or seventh year of our life affects our 20th or 30th or 40th year.

The other general reaction to the Middle Ages tends toward the opposite extreme. Instead of excising the Middle Ages from the body of the Church, this perspective fixes upon it as the archetype of Christian life. In response to the "bad things" which happened in the Middle Ages, proponents of this view say something along the lines of, "One has to take into account that people in the Middle Ages didn't have our modern values. We should not condemn them for things which may seem bad to us but which were for them quite normal."

This second perspective on the Middle Ages places the era on a pedestal, as it were. Advocates of this viewpoint make the Middle Ages a caricature of the truth, a syrupy distortion which lies in a mausoleum guarded by a perpetual flame and sweetened by the odor of incense.

These two perspectives on the Middle Ages represent, respectively, the extremes in Protestant and Catholic interpretations of the period. Fortunately these extremes exert less influence today than previously. Both Catholics and Protestants today are taking off the denominational blinders which for centuries kept them from looking at their collective medieval past with objectivity and reverence — with objectivity because we need to know and acknowledge the truth about ourselves, with reverence because we need to honor our ancestors in the faith who preserved and passed on to us the gospel of Jesus Christ.

In this book I attempt to speak of the medieval Church both objectively and reverently. My purpose is simply to describe the Middle Ages in itself, and not to present the era as an insignificant prelude to the Reformation.* I wish to present what I regard as the Church's grandest epoch, a time in which the Christian faith came close to winning for the gospel the hearts and minds of an entire civilization.

Acknowledgments

This is not a work of original scholarship, nor is it intended to be. I am not a professional scholar but a writer who greatly admires the scholars and attempts to make their conclusions available to the average reader. What I have done in the upcoming pages is to popularize the work of several experts in the fields of Church history and the history of Christian thought.

I am particularly indebted (as I was in the predecessor to this volume, *The People of the Creed*) to four masterpieces of scholarship and erudition: (1) Jaroslav Pelikan's four-volume *The Christian Tradition* (The University of Chicago Press, 1971); (2) Justo Gonzalez's three-volume *A History of Christian Thought* (Abingdon Press, 1971); (3) the 10-volume *History of the Church* edited by Hubert Jedin (originally *Handbuch der Kirchengeschichte*, English translation, 1965, Crossroad Publishing Co., 1982); and (4) Louis Bouyer's three-volume *A History of Christian Spirituality* (The Seabury Press, 1982).

---

* The flow of Christian history from the mid-15th century onward will be treated in two upcoming volumes, *The People of Anguish: The Story Behind the Reformation* and *The People of Hope: The Story Behind the Modern Church*.

The present volume then, in addition to being a popular introduction to the Church of the Middle Ages for the average reader, is also an introduction to the four works cited above, as well as to other scholarly treatises cited in the bibliographies of those works on which I have also relied. Finally, since Professor Pelikan's work in particular gives exhaustive annotations to the primary source material of medieval Christian literature, the present book will likewise serve as an introduction to those primary sources. Anyone wishing to travel farther on the road of medieval Church history than my introductory overview in this volume would permit, is encouraged to consult the four authorities cited above.

If the upcoming pages make available to the average reader the enormous contribution to our understanding of the Middle Ages achieved by the experts in the field, I will have been amply rewarded.

CONTENTS

TIMELINE: MIDDLE AGES (600-1450)

Secular Rulers	Events	Popes
	600 c. 600: Beginning of feudalism	Gregory I (the Great): 590-604
Heraclius (Byzantium: 610-641)	612: Muhammad establishes religion of Islam	
Isidore of Seville (636)		Honorius I (625-638)
		Severinus (640-640)
		John IV (640-642)
		Martin I (649-655)
Maximus the Confessor (662)		
	681: Council of Constantinople condemns Monotheletism	Leo II (681-683)
	700	
Leo III (Byzantium: 717-741)	c. 726: Byzantines begin policy of iconoclasm	
Venerable Bede (735)	732: Charles Martel repels Moslem invasion of Europe	
Constantine V (Byzantium: 741-775)		
Pepin the Short (Franks: 751-768)	Boniface (754)	
	756: Donation of Pepin establishes Papal States	Stephen II (752-757)
	787: Second Council of Nicaea condemns iconoclasm	
	800	
Charlemagne (Franks: 768-814)	794: Synod of Frankfort 796: Synod of Frejus 800: Charlemagne	
Irene (Byzantium: 797-802)	condemns Spanish defends use of "Roman Emperor"	Leo III (795-816)
Alcuin of York (804)	Adoptionism filioque	
Benedict of Aniane (821)		
Einhard (840)		
Louis I (the Pious; Franks: 814-840)	843: Holy Roman Empire divided among three of Louis I's sons; Byzantines restore use of icons	
	853: Gottschalk's positions on the Trinity and predestination are condemned	
Rabanus Maurus (856)		Nicholas I (858-867)
Radbertus (865)		Adrian II (867-872)
Ratramnus (868)		John VIII (872-882)
Erigena (877)		
Hincmar of Reims (882)		

900

1000

1100

Central timeline

- 910: Abbey of Cluny founded
- 962: Pope John XII crowns Otto I Holy Roman Emperor
- 994: Cluniac reform begins to spread across Europe
- 1000: Feudalism has evolved into complex societal system
- 1022: Synod of Pavia decrees strict celibacy for all orders of the Church
- 1054: Schism between Eastern and Western Churches
- 1066: Battle of Hastings: William of Normandy becomes king of England
- 1076: Pope Gregory VII excommunicates Henry IV
- 1078: Investiture controversy begins
- 1095-1099: First Crusade
- c.1095: *Chanson de Roland*
- 1098: Cistercian Order founded
- 1122: Concordat of Worms
- 1145: *The Sentences of Divinity* lists seven sacraments
- 1146-1147: Revolt of Arnold of Brescia
- 1147-1148: Second Crusade
- 1150: Peter Lombard's *Sentences*
- 1150-1250: Heyday of French troubadours
- 1160: *The Cid*
- c.1175: Peter Waldo begins preaching apostolic poverty
- 1178ff.: Albigensian heresy propagated
- 1140-1227: Goliardic poets flourish
- 1189-1192: Third Crusade

Popes

- John XII (955-964)
- Benedict VI (973-974)
- John XIV (983-984)
- Boniface VII (984-985)
- John XVI (anti-pope: 997-998)
- Gregory V (996-999)
- Benedict VIII (1012-1024)
- John XIX (1024-1033)
- Benedict IX (1033-1045)
- Gregory VI (1045-1046)
- Sylvester III (1045-1045)
- Clement II (1046-1047)
- Leo IX (1049-1054)
- Victor II (1055-1057)
- Gregory VII (Hildebrand: 1073-1085)
- Clement III (anti-pope: 1080, 1084-1100)
- Urban II (1088-1099)
- Paschal II (1099-1118)
- Calixtus II (1119-1124)
- Alexander III (1159-1181)

Rulers and figures

- Odo of Cluny (942)
- Otto I (Germany: 936-973)
- Otto II (Germany: 973-983)
- Otto III (Germany: 983-1002)
- Henry II (Germany: 1002-1024)
- Avicenna (1037)
- Conrad II (Germany: 1024-1039)
- Henry III (Germany: 1039-1056)
- Peter Damian (1072)
- William I (England: 1066-1087)
- Henry IV (Germany: 1056-1106)
- Alexius I (Byzantium: 1081-1118)
- Henry V (Germany: 1098-1125)
- Anselm of Canterbury (1098-1125)
- Peter Abelard (1142)
- Bernard of Clairvaux (1153)
- Peter Lombard (1160)
- Louis VII (France: 1137-1180)
- Frederick I (Barbarossa: Germany: 1152-1190)
- Hildegarde of Hesse (1179)
- Averroes (1189)
- Baldwin of Canterbury (1190)
- Richard I (the Lionhearted: England: 1189-1199)

Secular Rulers

Otto IV (Germany: 1198-1215)   Eleanor of Aquitaine (1204)
Philip II (Augustus; France: 1180-1225)
John (England: 1199-1216)   Dominic Guzman (1221)
Francis of Assisi (1226)   Stephen Langton (1228)
Frederick II (Sicily and Germany: 1194-1250)
Louis IX (France: 1226-1270)

Bonaventure (1274)   Thomas Aquinas (1274)
Siger of Brabant (1281)   Albert the Great (1280)
Rudolf (Germany: 1273-1291)   Roger Bacon (1292)
Edward I (England: 1272-1307)
John Duns Scotus (1308)
Philip IV (the Fair; France: 1285-1314)

Meister Eckhart (1327)
Philip VI (France: 1328-1350)
Marsilius of Padua (1342)   Ubertino of Casale (1341)
William of Ockham (1347)
Edward III (England: 1327-1377)

Petrarch (1374)
Catherine of Siena (1380)   Gerard Groote (1384)
John Wycliffe (1384)

John Hus (1415)   Julian of Norwich (1413)

Nicholas of Cusa (1464)
Thomas à Kempis (1471)

Timeline

1200

1200: Feudalism is on the decline   1202-1204: Fourth Crusade
1208: Francis founds Friars Minor; papal interdict on London
1215: Magna Carta; Fourth Lateran Council;   1217: Fifth Crusade
Order of Preachers founded by Dominic
1227: Beginning of papal Inquisition   1225: *Roman de la Rose* is begun
1204-1229: Albigensian Crusades

1274: Second Council of Lyons establishes doctrine of purgatory

1291: End of the Crusades
1295: Edward I's "Model Parliament"
1305: Beginning of the Babylonian Captivity of the papacy

1300

1337: Hundred Years' War begins
1347-1352: Black Death kills nearly a third of Europe

1377: Papacy returns to Rome   1378: Western Schism begins
1381: Peasants revolt in England

1400

1415: Hus burned at the stake;
Council of Constance condemns Wycliffe's doctrines
1431: Council of Basle; Joan of Arc burned at the stake
1438-1443: Council of Florence attempts to reunite Western and Eastern Churches
1453: Constantinople falls to Moslems; Hundred Years' War ends;
Gutenberg's movable type

1483: Martin Luther is born

Popes

Innocent III (1198-1216)
Honorius III (1216-1227)
Gregory IX (1227-1241)
Innocent IV (1243-1254)
Urban IV (1261-1264)
Clement IV (1265-1268)

Boniface VIII (1294-1303)
Clement V (1305-1314)

John XXII (1316-1334)
Benedict XII (1334-1342)
Clement VI (1342-1352)
Innocent VI (1352-1362)
Urban V (1362-1370)
Gregory XI (1370-1378)
Urban VI (1378-1389)
Clement VII (anti-pope: 1378-1394)
Boniface IX (1389-1404)
Innocent VII (1404-1406)
Alexander V (anti-pope: 1409-1410)
Gregory XII (1406-1415)
Benedict XIII (anti-pope: 1394-1423)
Martin V (1417-1431)
Eugene IV (1431-1447)

John XXIII (anti-pope: 1410-1415)

Single dates in parentheses indicate an individual's date of death; dates spanning a number of years refer to time in office.

INTRODUCTION

From Adolescence to Young Adulthood

By way of metaphor we could say that this book is about a person—the Christian Church as it existed during the period from about 600 A.D. to about 1450. In *The People of the Creed: The Story Behind the Early Church*, we left that person at the end of the sixth century—at the close of an era characterized by the fractured unity of the defunct Roman Empire—standing on the verge of a new and uncertain era in life. Continuing the metaphor, we could say that in *The People of the Creed* we considered the life of this person until about the onset of adolescence. Now, as we begin the story of the medieval Church, we will continue our friend's personal history through adolescence to the onset of young adulthood: from about age 13 to about age 19.

This metaphor is not unrelated to the way in which medieval Christians looked at themselves. The very term *middle ages* reflected their belief that they were somehow living in an age that was incomplete, a transition to a more mature epoch. Thus a seventh-century bishop referred to his era as the "middle ages" which came between the First and Second Coming of Christ. Albert the Great in the 13th century likewise spoke of "the middle age" in which Christians must struggle with evil. Since medieval Christians themselves regarded their age as one of growth, as a time which looked for completion, they would perhaps not object to our referring to them as maturing adolescents struggling with the onset of adulthood.

As we know from our own experience of adolescence, the years between 13 and 19 are difficult. They are years in which our major thrust in life is to integrate the three constituent elements of our personality: behavior, intellectual development and what we could call "innermost self"—that part of our being where we most truly define ourselves as "I."

To tell the personal story of the medieval Church by focusing only on its external behavior (the *events* of medieval Christian history) would thus not express the entire story of the Church's struggle to grow through adolescence to young adulthood. To present an accurate picture, we must also discuss the Church's intellectual growth (the history of medieval Christian thought), as well as our adolescent's struggle to define "who I truly am" (the history of medieval Christian faith).

As we did in *The People of the Creed*, then, we will categorize our discussion in this book into events, thought and belief, and we will likewise focus more on the history of thought than on the history of events. The third element to our story—belief—is *the* element which most clearly defines the Church of the Middle Ages, so much so that we will give a new meaning to the word *faith*.

The early Church defined faith as normative doctrine formalized in the great Creeds. In the Middle Ages the quest for faith becomes much more—a search not just for knowledge *about* God (as we could characterize the early Church's quest to formalize the Creeds), but a search for knowledge *of* God. The child of the early Church now has become a restless young adult who wants to *experience* God.

In telling this tripartite story of events, thought and faith, we will notice that—like most awkward, uncoordinated and self-conscious adolescents—the medieval Church is frequently out of kilter. It has a difficult time integrating its behavior with its thought and with its faith. On the surface—where we discuss events—we will find that the medieval Church is often belligerent and destructive, even superstitious and corrupt. If we were to stop with externals we could understand why many people look upon the medieval Church as a mere way station on the road to the Reformation.

Yet as we probe deeper we will find that the adolescent's often intolerable conduct is not the entire story. We will find in the Church of the Middle Ages achievements of thought and experiences of faith which stamp this as a period of Christian greatness, as an era with its own identity, and not as a loose collection of horrid events which necessitate the Reformation.

In the Middle Ages the Church is trying to "get it all together"—behavior, intellectual maturation and faith. It partially succeeds and partially fails.

The story of the Middle Ages engages us in a story of the

Church's quest for wholeness. In the end complete wholeness is not achieved. Yet it is the very quest for wholeness and the legacy of this quest which make the story behind the Church of the Middle Ages remarkable and unique.

THE QUEST FOR WHOLENESS: EVENTS, THOUGHT, FAITH

In order to clarify what we mean by "the quest for wholeness," let's take an introductory look at our three categories of events, thought and faith.

The Events

In looking at this first category, we find everywhere in the events of the Middle Ages a desire on the part of Christians to achieve *external* wholeness. Let's look at three examples of this.

1) The Attempt to Reestablish Empire. The most obvious example of the quest for external wholeness was the attempt to reestablish (or reclaim) the fallen Roman Empire. The unification of the western half of the fallen empire was undertaken by the Germanic tribes which had succeeded the former Western Roman emperors in political leadership. A king of one of these Germanic tribes, Charlemagne of the Franks, was crowned "Roman Emperor" by Pope Leo III in the year 800.

Yet during the time of Charlemagne's "imperial rule" there already existed in Constantinople (today's Istanbul) persons who claimed that *they* were Roman emperors. These persons were the Byzantine emperors, or rulers of the "Byzantine Empire"—the Eastern Greek civilization which asserted the prerogatives of the ancient Roman Empire for a thousand years after the last Roman emperor in the West had succumbed to the barbarian invasions.

During the very times when German kings were claiming to be emperors of the entire Christian world, Byzantine enclaves continued in the West (in Sicily and southern Italy, for example). Yet the Byzantines could hardly claim to have restored the ancient Roman Empire either since they lived in nearly constant danger of Moslem invasion.

Obviously, then, the claim of empire was specious, whether asserted by German kings or by Byzantines, but the claim was made nonetheless.* As we shall see, the effects of this dual claim to empire

---

* The Western Empire eventually came to be called The Holy Roman Empire, although as Voltaire once wrote, it was neither holy, Roman nor an empire.

was to have great effect on the external life of the medieval Christian Church. As in *The People of the Creed*, we will find that tensions between Western and Eastern Christians had a lot to do with the history of the period we are exploring.

2) The Attempt to Establish Unified Christian Authority. A second example of the medieval Church's quest for external wholeness was the struggle by the medieval popes to establish themselves as the sole authoritative spokesmen for normative Christian doctrine. But their efforts met resistance, as in the earliest Christian centuries, from the bishops of the East who resented Rome's claim to papal primacy.

During the Middle Ages, however, the greater challenge to Rome's claim to papal primacy came not from other bishops, but from Western political rulers who considered themselves authorized to establish Church policy in the lands which they ruled. To counter this challenge the medieval popes entered into the political arena as never before, confronting the secular rulers of their day to such an extent that the popes themselves *became* secular politicans. In the pages ahead we will witness constant competition between pope and prince for the control of Western Christianity.

3) The Attempt to Preserve Christian Society in the Face of Islam. Although popes fought constantly with Western rulers, and although the Eastern Church rejected the popes' claim to primacy, all Christians agreed that a united effort should be made to counter the spread of the new religion of Islam. The establishment of Islam (the word means "submission") by the Arab prophet Muhammad (in 612) constituted the most significant event of the early Middle Ages.

By the year 732 the Moslems had either converted to their new faith or subjugated to their political rule peoples of the Middle East, North Africa, Spain and portions of southern France. In this vast sea of Islam the Byzantine Empire resembled tiny patches of seaweed clustered in what is today Turkey, the Balkans, Sicily, southern and central Italy, Sardinia and Corsica (see map, p. 5). Western imperial" society, on the other hand, had not even begun to coalesce into recognizable shape by this time. Christians in both West and East were virtually surrounded by a new and (it seemed to millions) more vibrant religion, culture and society.

The onslaught of Islam and the counterattack of Christianity played a significant role in the story of the medieval Church's quest for external wholeness—especially, as we shall see, in the episode known as the Crusades.

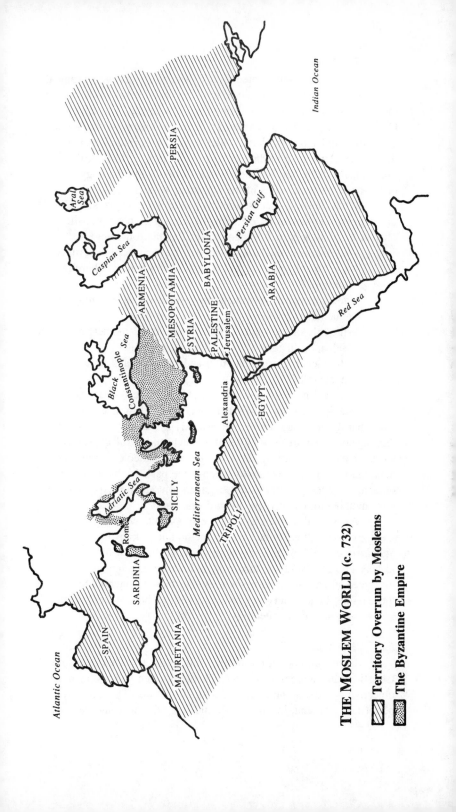

THE MOSLEM WORLD (c. 732)

Territory Overrun by Moslems

The Byzantine Empire

The Thought

Just as Christians wanted to establish political and geographical wholeness, so too they wanted to create a world in which Christian thought was homogeneous and universally accepted. Our study of Christian thought in the pages ahead will thus be a study of the Church's quest for intellectual wholeness. *Theology* comes into clearer focus in the Middle Ages than in the early Christian period. In fact, the desire to establish a stable, unified and universally applicable theology is one of the chief characteristics of the Christian Middle Ages.

What questions were studied by medieval theologians? We could not begin to enumerate all of them. In the pages ahead we will look only at the most significant themes, such as the following:

— the nature of God as expressed in the doctrine of the Trinity;
— the nature, purpose and boundaries of earthly Church authority;
— the concept of sacrament and especially the meaning of the Eucharist;
— the role of the saints—particularly Jesus' mother, Mary—in salvation history;
— the meaning of redemption and salvation and how they are accomplished;
— the definition of heresy and the Church's response to heresy.

Theology during the first five centuries of the medieval period could hardly be called innovative. Rather, it was very conservative, seeking not to venture into new territory but to address all questions in terms of past authority. In the East, Byzantine theology really never departed from this tendency to sanctify the past. In the West, on the other hand, theologians gradually began to adjust their perspective, alter their methodology and move toward originality.

As we follow the changing developments within Western theology, we will encounter a new methodology known as *Scholasticism*. Scholasticism was an attempt to bring the forces of reason to bear upon the study of theology. Scholastic theologians frequently disagreed on substantive issues while using the same methods to analyze those issues. Scholasticism therefore was not a school of theology but a new way of "doing" theology.

The Faith

Christian thought during the Middle Ages spilled over into Christian faith in countless ways. Theology often had a very practical objective—to define normative Christian doctrine. This objective so permeated Christian life in the Middle Ages that it would be accurate simply to equate the developing doctrine with the faith of medieval Christianity. That is one reason (though not the only one) why the title of this book is not *The People of Faith* but *The People of* the *Faith*. In order to acquire a well-rounded concept of medieval Christianity, we need to explore three aspects of "the faith."

1) The Faith as Objective Doctrine. Through the efforts of Christian thinkers, theology formed a body of doctrine which was promulgated as the core of the Christian faith. The faith itself became in the Middle Ages something to be venerated and revered. (The name of our American city Santa Fe—"Holy Faith"—testified in later centuries to this idea.)

On the one hand the medieval concept of "the faith" was frequently static; that is, the faith became an "it" to be found and accepted, or a body of doctrine with which one aligned oneself in order to achieve salvation. The arbiter of orthodox faith was the hierarchical Church—in the West especially, the supreme pontiff, the pope.

Although held up as an ideal in the Middle Ages, this concept of the faith as a static, fixed, universally accepted body of doctrine was never really achieved. Beneath the surface of the solid rock of doctrine which "the one, true faith" was supposed to be, there was a constant percolation of doubts, questions and dissent.

Popes themselves were found to take erroneous positions on points of doctrine (see pp. 68-69 and 132, for example), and the most respected thinkers often departed from the common faith on various points. Thus the faith—though on the surface fixed, immutable and irrevocably established as an objective body of doctrine—had a more pliable and subjective dimension to it which we must also study.

2) The 'Everyday Faith.' People in the Middle Ages had a tremendous desire to make the faith *tangible*, something of practical value in their daily lives. The sacraments of the Church were, of course, an obvious means for achieving this. Medieval thinkers constantly affirmed that Christianity is an experience of God's grace manifested in realities which can be touched, tasted and felt.

Yet the sacraments did not suffice for ordinary medieval Christians. They looked for and developed other ways to make the faith tangible—that is, to make it less of an objective body of doctrine and more of a subjective and sensate experience. Since ordinary Christians did not participate in the great theological debates over doctrine, they turned to more earthy ways of understanding and experiencing the faith. We can call this impulse on the part of ordinary believers to bring heaven closer to earth "everyday faith."

In the pages ahead we will observe how medieval Christians

7

venerated relics, developed the cult of the saints, undertook pilgrimages to holy shrines, saw miraculous interventions of God's power in their everyday lives, tried to control the spirits of good and evil—in short, how they superimposed their own folk mentality upon the "official" body of doctrine.

3) The Faith as Contemplative Mystical Experience. In addition to the everyday faith, another impulse within medieval Christian life was at work to make the faith more subjective and personal, to establish wholeness, but on a much deeper level. This deeper dimension of the quest for wholeness, represented by the soul's desire for spiritual union with God, achieved majestic expression in the growth of the contemplative tradition.

Just as our study of the history of medieval Christian thought will lead us to *theology*, so our study of the medieval Church's contemplative tradition will lead us to *spirituality*. While theology tends toward the *definition* of doctrine, spirituality emphasizes the *effect* doctrine has in the Christian's life, and especially in the Christian's innermost consciousness.

Medieval spirituality is best understood in terms of two words that are increasingly alien to the 20th century—*contemplation* and *mysticism*. What contemplation and mysticism meant during the Middle Ages is not always easy to determine, because different spiritual writers used the terms in different ways.

As a working definition we could define contemplation as the soul's union with God in silent prayer. Some medieval Christians looked upon contemplation as a sensate phenomenon in which one experienced great emotional fervor manifested, for example, in the outpouring of tears; others, however, looked upon contemplation as totally transcendent to sense experience. A mystic can be defined as someone who experiences a virtually permanent state of contemplation, as if contemplation were a part of his or her personality. (Recall Paul's words in 1 Thessalonians 5:17 to "never cease praying.")

In the Byzantine East, contemplation and mysticism were integral parts of everyday spirituality. Eastern Christians seemed to take to the interior life by natural disposition. In the West, however, Christians took a more studied approach to spirituality, relying on the guidance and experience not only of St. Augustine and other Western Fathers, but also on the writings of Eastern spiritual masters, such as the anonymous writer known as Pseudo-Dionysius.

8

'ANIMA' AND 'ANIMUS':
20TH-CENTURY MODEL FOR THE MEDIEVAL QUEST

Contemplative spirituality helped people become whole in two senses: First, it enabled Christians to experience God's wholeness within their own hearts; second, because of this experience of intimate union with God, Christians became more whole and integrated in their own personalities.

In 20th-century terminology, medieval spirituality provided a means for the integration within each individual of what psychologist Carl Jung has called the *animus* and *anima*, the male and female psychological traits which lie polarized within each human being. According to Jung, until each person harmonizes within his or her own personality the *animus* and the *anima*, he or she cannot be said truly

The prominence of this notion of integrative personal wholeness during the Middle Ages is seen most strikingly in the medieval man's appreciation of the traditional feminine personality traits, and in the respect shown by him for femininity and womanhood. For the first time in human history men sought to develop such traditionally feminine virtues as intuition, receptivity, synthesis, flexibility and, above all, romantic love. The Middle Ages were a time in which feeling, sensitivity and civility for the first time dominated many men's lives.

Yet the experience of feminine energy in the Middle Ages—or the development of the *anima*—did not affect all men in the same way, especially men in the Church. Joan of Arc, a woman who epitomized the synthesis of *animus* and *anima* as well as anyone in the Middle Ages, was burned at the stake by churchmen who thought her to be a witch. Bernard of Clairvaux, a male who epitomized in many respects the harmony of *animus* and *anima*, could yet urge a crowd of bloodthirsty knights to kill Moslems for Christ.

Thus, the Middle Ages' quest for wholeness produced the most striking paradoxes and contradictions. At one pole of the spectrum of medieval Christian consciousness stood the masculine thrust for dominance, best represented in the institutional Church and its growing quest for worldly power. At the other extreme stood the intuitive receptivity of Christian feminism, best represented by contemplative spirituality and the burgeoning devotion to Mary, the mother of Jesus. The most urgent question faced by the late medieval Church was whether these two poles of experience could be reconciled and brought into an integrated whole.

The medieval Church's quest for wholeness was thus dominated by the tension between masculine and feminine energies circulating throughout medieval society. Again and again medieval spirituality challenged the institutional structure of the Church (the Church's *animus*) to harmonize itself with the feminine energy activated by the contemplative, mystical and devotional movements (the Church's *anima*). Could the institutional Church harness and synthesize these two forms of energy, or would it retreat fearfully into reliance on perverted extremes of the male psychological traits—domination, oppression and brutality?

This duality between *animus* and *anima* best summarizes many characteristics of the events, thought and faith which we will study in this book.

CHAPTER ONE

DAWN OF THE CHRISTIAN MIDDLE AGES

From Gregory the Great to Charlemagne (604-800)

T o begin, let us survey the external configuration of early medieval society from the death of Pope Gregory the Great (604) to the coronation of Charlemagne as Roman emperor (800). We will focus on three major categories of events: the interaction of the papacy and secular powers, developments in the Byzantine Empire and the confrontation between Islam and Christianity.

THE PAPACY AND THE SECULAR POWERS

After the collapse of Roman rule in the Western Empire, northern Italy fell under the domination of a barbarian tribe known as the Lombards. The Lombards made their capital at Pavia, some 200 miles north of Rome (see map, p. 14). Between Pavia and Rome, on the Adriatic Sea, stood Ravenna, the Italian headquarters of the Byzantine Empire. The popes remained in Rome (which technically lay within Byzantine territory) ruling the dried-up shell of the former capital of the Western Empire. Italy, then, was a graphic sign of the West's state of disunity: three separate capitals under the control of three separate authorities—the Lombard king at Pavia, the Byzantine emperor's legate at Ravenna and the pope in Rome.

This situation created a great deal of political tension as well as a great deal of maneuvering by those who controlled the three centers of power. Under Pope Gregory the Great, Lombard power was held in check in Italy. Gregory became a clever secular ruler, boldly challenging

THE LOMBARDS IN ITALY (c. 600)

Lombard Kingdom and Duchies

Byzantine Territory

Lombard attempts to unify Italy. He did this by reconciling Rome with Constantinople, so that the ancient forces of empire thwarted the Lombard threat. Constantinople sent Gregory money to pay Byzantine soldiers in the West, and Gregory was given a free hand by the Byzantines to appoint governors and generals in Italy.

Deteriorating Relations Between East and West

After Pope Gregory's time, however, the papacy became increasingly alienated from the Byzantines, largely because of continued Christological quarrels stemming from unresolved conflicts (discussed in *The People of the Creed*). Rome disagreed with the actions taken at certain Church councils in the East, and this led to the breakup of the tenuous concord between East and West which Gregory had established. Pope Martin I (649-655) was actually arrested by the Byzantine legate in Italy and transported to the East where he died a humiliated captive.

Under Byzantine Emperor Leo III (717-741), the relationship between Rome and Constantinople deteriorated still further. Emperor Leo went so far as to impose taxes on lands owned by the popes. When the *iconoclast controversy* broke out in the East (as we shall discuss shortly), Pope Gregory III excommunicated Emperor Leo. Continuing theological controversies between East and West provided each side ample opportunity to seek political advantage over the other.

A New Papal Protector

With the popes and the Byzantines at each other's throats, the Lombard kings felt confident to consolidate their grip on Italy. When the Lombard King Aistulf began to emerge as a greater threat to papal power than the Byzantines had been, the popes went shopping for a protector. In 753, Pope Stephen II traveled across the Alps to secure the aid of Pepin the Short, king of the Germanic tribe known as the Franks. Pepin's father, Charles Martel, had previously ousted a rival line of Frankish rulers (the Merovingians) and had established the Carolingian line (named after Charles—"Carolus"—Martel).

Pope Stephen entreated King Pepin to win back for the papacy all the lands in Italy which the Lombards had taken. Such a request had great appeal to a barbarian ruler like Pepin, who saw the pope as the heir of ancient Roman power and prestige. Further, because Pepin and his family were Christians, it seemed a sign of God's favor when St. Peter's successor personally appealed to him for aid. Pepin eagerly accepted the Pope's request and set out with his troops for Italy.

In 756 Pepin defeated the Lombard King Aistulf. In a formal "deed" known as the *Donation of Pepin*, the Frankish king gave to the pope a wide strip of territories across central Italy ("the Papal States"), some of which were claimed by the Byzantines.

The *Donation of Pepin* accomplished two things: (1) It brought the Carolingians into Italy as the papacy's special protectors. (2) It infuriated the Byzantines and further alienated them from the West. How, the Byzantines demanded, could an upstart barbarian chieftain dare to convey "imperial" land to the pope?

A New 'Empire'

Byzantine anger reached its climax in the year 800 when Pepin's son, Charlemagne, was crowned "Roman Emperor" by Pope Leo III in a solemn ceremony in Rome. Pope Leo's policy of dating papal documents according to the years of Charlemagne's rule graphically illustrated the alliance between the papacy and the Carolingians—and the increasing submission of the papacy to the new secular power. Previously the popes had dated their decretals according to their own years in office.

The message was clear: The papacy had surrendered much of its temporal sovereignty to the emperor. This development marked the beginning of what was to become a constant struggle all during the Middle Ages between the pope and the Western emperor for the mastery of Western Christendom.

THE BYZANTINE EMPIRE
TO THE TIME OF EMPRESS IRENE

Justinian the Great (483-565) had served as emperor of the Byzantine state during a time marred by constant theological controversy. As we saw in *The People of the Creed* (p. 103), Justinian himself was a capable theologian, but had been unsuccessful in reconciling the heretical Monophysite party with those who supported the Council of Chalcedon (451). Justinian's followers on the imperial throne were no more successful than he in preventing Christological controversy in the East.

Further, under increasing assault from the Moslems, the Byzantine Empire became cut off from regular contact with the West and turned more and more in upon itself. By the end of the reign of Emperor Heraclius I (610-641), Byzantium was already showing signs of the conservative Greek introversion which was to characterize Byzantine life all during the Middle Ages.

Byzantine Civilization

Since the bulk of this book will focus on the Western Church, we should acknowledge at the outset how greatly the bias of our Western hindsight colors our understanding of Byzantine history. Well into the late Middle Ages, Byzantine civilization was greatly superior to that of the West. When Paris was but a mud hole surrounded by crude barbarian huts, Constantinople was a magnificent metropolis with dozens of museums and libraries and over 400 beautifully adorned churches.

Throughout the Middle Ages Byzantium was to remain a mystery to the adolescent West. Byzantines, on the other hand, felt themselves infinitely superior to "the godless souls in the deep hell of ignorance," as one Eastern theologian characterized the Latins.

Yet Byzantium's cultural elegance and its penchant for speculative theology could not prevent the Easterners from disagreeing violently among themselves as to what constituted orthodox Christianity. And in a state where the secular and the sacred were completely intermingled, the struggle to define doctrine inevitably led to political turmoil.

The best example of this is the *iconoclast controversy*.

The Iconoclast Controversy

Images and icons (pictures and statues of Jesus, Mary and the saints) had long been a staple of Byzantine spirituality. By the time of Byzantine Emperor Leo III (717-741), Christians in the East were attributing all sorts of miraculous powers to icons. In many places superstition had overtaken authentic Christian devotion. We will discuss the theological aspects of the iconoclast controversy in the next chapter. Here we are concerned only with the political storm unleashed when Emperor Leo attempted to suppress the use of icons in Christian worship.

By taking this fateful step, Leo polarized various elements within Byzantine Church and society. The principal supporters of icons were the monks, who not only relied on icons in their liturgies but also had a lucrative trade in icons. For many monasteries the manufacture of icons was the sole means of support. Since Byzantine society regarded monasticism as the highest ideal of Christian life, many of Emperor Leo's subjects violently resisted his attempts to prevent the monks' making of icons and the use of icons in the liturgy. Leo's policy came to be called *iconoclasm* — the "breaking of icons." When Leo removed a famous icon of Christ from the gate to the imperial palace, it provoked a riot which nearly toppled Leo's government.

Leo's son and successor, Emperor Constantine V (741-775), followed his father's practice. Constantine convened a bishops' synod in 754 which condemned both the production and veneration of icons; he vigorously enforced his iconoclast policy by closing and confiscating monasteries and by torturing monks and nuns. While the people solidly supported the monks, the army and most Byzantine bishops steadfastly obeyed the emperor, although various patriarchs (chief bishops) of Constantinople resisted the emperor's iconoclastic policy.

Political Intrigue in the Byzantine Court

After numerous plots and attempted coups, the emperor's enemies managed to eradicate him and his hated iconoclasm. This development was the beginning of the court intrigue which was to become a characteristic of Byzantine political life. To this very day the word *Byzantine* is defined in dictionaries as "characterized by a devious and usually surreptitious manner of operation."

The epitome of this dictionary definition was Irene, mother of Constantine VI, who became empress in 780. She schemed and intrigued her way into control of the government. Seeking to end the strife over the iconoclast controversy—which almost daily threatened to destroy Byzantine imperial rule—Irene convened the Second Council of Nicaea in 787, which reversed the previous imperial policy. The council condemned iconoclasm as a heresy and thus upheld the veneration of icons as orthodox Christian devotion.

The setback for the iconoclasts was a great victory for the Eastern monks, who from this moment on gained more and more power and prestige in Byzantine society—some even winning a certain degree of independence from Eastern bishops in Church affairs. Irene's supremacy, however, was short-lived. Outschemed by a more skillful group of schemers in her court, she was deposed by a party loyal to the new emperor, Nicephorus I (802-811), but not before she had blinded her own son, Constantine VI, as she vainly sought to prevent the very type of palace revolution which led to her demise.

The Islam-Christian Confrontation

About the year 612 an Arab caravan merchant named Muhammad (570-632) began the transformation of the entire shape of the Christian world. Having studied both the Old and New Testament, and having regularly dialogued in his mercantile business with Jews and Christians, Muhammad came to believe that he was receiving from God a direct call to transform and fulfill both Judaism and Christianity by preaching a new religion called *Islam*. Muhammad taught that he, like Moses and Jesus, was a prophet, but different from his predecessors in that he was the final prophet, revealing God's word in its most excellent form.

When Muhammad died he was succeeded by men called *caliphs* who envisioned Islam as a religion of conquest. Through the *jihad* ("holy war") they attempted to convert the infidels (Christians, Jews and all others) to the one, true religion of Islam. The caliphs were spectacularly successful.

In the mid-seventh century the Moslems drove the Byzantines from Syria and Palestine and defeated and converted the Persians in today's Iran and Iraq. In 669 the Moslems besieged Constantinople itself. The Byzantines repulsed the invaders through the use of a mysterious weapon known as "Greek fire," a chemical substance of unknown ingredients which was poured out from tubes and caught fire as soon as it landed on the water around the Moslem ships. For centuries only Greek fire kept the Byzantine capital safe from Moslem capture.

Egypt, however, was easy prey for the Moslems. Alexandria fell perhaps because of a fifth-column movement within the city led by disgruntled Monophysites who favored Muhammad's uncompromising monotheism over the Chalcedonians' Trinitarianism. (See *The People of the Creed*, Chapter 7.) The rest of North Africa fell swiftly. In 698 Carthage, the ancient capital of North African Christianity in the West, was taken by the invaders, who allied themselves with the native Berber tribesmen against the Christian population. From Carthage the Moslems prepared an attack on Christian Europe by massing their forces for the passage across the Mediterranean to Spain.

By 712 the former Visigothic capitals of Cordoba and Toledo had been captured, and the Moslems found themselves in control of all southern Spain. In 717 Moslem forces swept through northern Spain, crossed the Pyrenees and captured Narbonne in southern France. All of Frankish Europe now lay before the Moslem horde.

Had the Moslems been able to sweep across central Europe and advance toward Constantinople from the West, linking up with their brothers in the East who still regularly battered Constantinople's gates, there can be little doubt that all of Christian Europe would have been converted to Islam. Yet the Moslems were finally stopped in 732, near today's Tours in central France, by Charles Martel, the Carolingian patriarch and grandfather of Charlemagne.

Meanwhile, dissension and civil war had broken out within the Moslem ranks. Two distinct Moslem caliphates emerged: the Abbasid, which ruled in the East, and the Omayyad, which had already established itself in Spain. By 750 the focus of Moslem power shifted back to the East. The Omayyads in Spain were largely cut off from the Abbasids, who in 762 moved the Moslem capital even farther east, from Damascus to Baghdad. The Omayyad dynasty's crusading days in Spain ended scarcely half a century after they had begun. Yet the Omayyads stayed on in Spain, transforming their crusading fervor into an attitude of accommodation with the Spanish Christians.

Gradually the Moslems in Spain retreated entirely into the south. Until about the 11th century roughly the southern half of Spain was Moslem and the northern half Christian. During the time of Carolingian supremacy in Western Europe, the Moslem Caliph of Cordoba, Abd-er-Rahman II (822-852), built a civilization of art, literature and learning that outshone anything produced in Christian Europe. Significantly, the caliph granted freedom of worship to all—Jews and Christians alike—an act of tolerance which medieval Christians never reciprocated. We will pick up the remaining story of Christianity's conflict with Islam beginning on page 88, when we discuss the Crusades.

Now that we have sketched the major events of the early medieval period, let us discuss the elements of thought and faith that characterized this era.

THEOLOGY AND SPIRITUALITY: REVERENCE FOR THE PAST

Between the death of Pope Gregory the Great in 604 and Charlemagne's imperial rule (800-814), there was little creative theology undertaken in either East or West. The early medieval thinkers were, for the most part, preservers of the past.

Writing in the East, Maximus the Confessor (580-662), "the father of Byzantine theology," often stressed his reliance on the Greek Fathers. For Maximus, any theological discussion required "the voices of the Fathers as evidence for the faith of the Church."[1]

In the West, too, theological writing relied heavily on the Fathers—and especially on *the* Father, Augustine. The English monk known as the Venerable Bede (673-735), for example, referred to himself not as a scholar or a teacher but as a "compiler," and in this statement he was accurate. Most of what Bede and other Western theologians wrote was drawn from Jerome, Ambrose, Gregory and Augustine.

If the early medieval thinkers were largely preservers of the past, what was it that they sought to preserve? The answer depended upon whether one was an Easterner or a Westerner. The tradition which each side of the Church sought to preserve differed as one passed from East to West.

Eastern Theological Tendencies

In the East, Maximus the Confessor and other Byzantine writers elaborated upon an idea long cherished in Eastern thought: the concept of salvation as deification. This idea had been prominent in several of the Greek Fathers, particularly Clement of Alexandria and Athanasius. (See *The People of the Creed*, p. 72.)

Maximus and other Easterners relied heavily on such Scripture passages as John 10:34 ("I have said, You are Gods") and 2 Peter 1:4 ("...you...might become sharers of the divine nature") to develop this aspect of traditional Byzantine theology. Maximus frequently repeated Clement of Alexandria's and Athanasius' teaching that "God became man so that man may learn how to become God."

How does one become "deified"? Maximus had several answers. First, through reading Scripture "we are purified and illumined for the sacred birth from God."[2] Second, through the sacraments "we are made perfect in knowledge."[3] Finally, through contemplation the human mind is raised to the mind of Christ. Thus, Byzantine theology effortlessly spilled over into spirituality.

This was to be a constant characteristic of Byzantine theology. No theological conclusion was made for its own sake; rather, the purpose of Byzantine theology was to produce in the individual Christian's consciousness the direct experience of what was being proposed. Byzantine theology was thus at the same time *mystagogy*—that is, the attempt to initiate Christians into mystical experience. Maximus, for example, defined his theology as "mystagogy through knowledge."

There thus developed in Byzantine theology an emphasis on a type of knowledge that is beyond reason and analysis. The founder of this Byzantine theological tendency was Pseudo-Dionysius (early sixth century; see *The People of the Creed*, p. 119). Pseudo-Dionysius said that one can only say what God is not, not what God is. Maximus and the Byzantines (and eventually some Western theologians, too) took up this concept of God's mysterious "unknown-ness" and developed the "apophatic" school of theology—that is, a theology based on negation. By negation, Pseudo-Dionysius, Maximus and other Byzantines did not mean that nothing true can be said about God, but that God as he is in himself is beyond human knowledge.

Maximus relied on such passages as John 1:18 ("No one has ever seen God") to explain how it is that theology cannot truly encompass God. Theology can only see God's *effects* in the world, Maximus said, in the same way that the apostles on Mt. Tabor saw not God but the *glory* of God when Jesus was transfigured before them. Maximus concluded, therefore, that "a perfect mind is one which, by *true faith*,

21

in supreme ignorance knows the supremely unknowable one."[4]

Here Maximus was speaking of faith as a type of psychological process—"supreme ignorance"—by which one comes to know God. By defining theology in terms of "ignorance about God," Maximus was affirming that ultimately what we *experience* of God will constantly transcend revealed truth, because words cannot limit God's nature. This thrust toward the subjective in Maximus's theology was to be of great significance for later Western theologians as they gradually started reading Eastern sources (see p. 158 ff.).

Early Western Theology

Early medieval thinkers in the West were not ignorant of the mystical thrust of theology. Abbot Isidore of Seville (560-636), for example, showed his similarity to Maximus when he wrote, "God is known correctly only when we deny that he can be known perfectly."[5] Yet, by and large, Western theology at this state of its development did not venture as far into the realm of apophatic theology as did Byzantine thought.

Western thinkers were so wary of deviating from anything "the divine Augustine" had said that they simply tracked the great Father's teachings. Consequently, since Augustine had been challenged as bishop to resolve so many practical issues, early medieval Western thinkers mirrored his more objective and practical approach.

A good example of this is found in the sermons of the English missionary to Germany, Boniface (680-754). Boniface stressed a practical, everyday theology based on the imitation of Jesus' early life. Boniface defined salvation not as deification but as "obeying the commandments of God and always doing single-mindedly the will of Him who 'desires all men to be saved' and none to perish."[6]

This close connection between theology and morality in the West was necessitated by the Church's effort to overcome the crude paganism of the barbarian tribes to whom missionaries such as Boniface preached the gospel. The Byzantines' highly speculative theology would have ill-served such men as Boniface.

Largely because of the practical need of the West for a theology that would transform the barbarians' behavior according to Christian morality, Western theologians spent much of their time talking about "spiritual merit" and how one achieved it. Consequently, it became very important to discuss the means by which a person received grace.

For Western thinkers the means of grace were several. Bede stressed the necessity of listening to the Word of God. As he put it, "The pastors of the Church have been ordained primarily for the task of preaching."[7] Charlemagne's court tutor, Alcuin of York (735-804), later echoed Bede when he wrote to a bishop, "This is your everlasting praise and glory, that you preach the Word of God to all with great confidence."[8]

Along with the preached Scriptures, the sacraments were another essential means of grace. Still in a state of evolution during this period, the sacraments had not yet solidified into the seven which are defined today. Bede, for example, did not consider Penance as a sacrament. Following Augustine, Western theologians during this early period stressed the centrality of Baptism. In later centuries, however, there was a shift in emphasis from Baptism to the Eucharist as the most important sacrament.

Obviously, the idea of spiritual merit played a big role in leading Western theologians to speak of purgatory, which Bede defined as "the place in which the souls of those in the hour of death take refuge in penance and are examined and chastised."[9] This notion clashed with the Eastern view of salvation as deification, where a state of purgation was seen as unnecessary once the soul's union with God had been effected here on earth. The West's teaching on purgatory was one of the main reasons why Eastern theologians looked upon the Latins' theology with suspicion.

Finally, true to Augustinian form, early Western medieval thinkers wrote a great deal about the Church, drawing nearly all their ideas from Augustine's *City of God*. The Church was referred to repeatedly as "God's city on earth" and his "kingdom." Bede wrote that Christ and the Church are "of one nature," and he reflected on the analogy between Jesus' teaching from Peter's boat (see Luke 5:3) and the pope's teaching from the "authority of the Church." Thus, even though Bede could write that "all those who have been elected by grace are called priests,"[10] he and other Western thinkers often commented on the need for a hierarchical structure in the Church.

One Westerner called the pope "the heavenly wielder of the keys who throws open the gates of heaven."[11] Bishop Isidore of Seville referred to the pope as the "chief of priests...the highest priest."[12] Hincmar (860-882), Archbishop of Reims, a staunch proponent of episcopal independence, could yet write, "the solicitude for all the Churches has been committed to the Holy Roman Church in Peter, the prince of the apostles."[13]

Early Medieval Spirituality

Despite the different emphases in Eastern and Western theology, we can nonetheless draw a common conclusion about Eastern and

Western *spirituality* down to the ninth century: Early medieval spirituality was overwhelmingly biblical and monastic. Lay spirituality apart from contact with the monastic life did not really exist in the West; and in the East, lay spirituality was so influenced by monasticism as to be incapable of its own development. Further, the Bible was the starting point for the monks' life of contemplation. For example, Bede defined contemplation as "tasting the consolation of the scriptures," and spiritual masters of both East and West stressed meditating fervently on Jesus' earthly life revealed in Scripture as the pathway to contemplative prayer.

Having discussed the differing theological starting points taken by Western and Eastern theologians, and having seen how the competing claims of empire led to tension between Rome and Constantinople, we will now resume the story of the Eastern and Western Empires' struggle to consolidate their power.

CHAPTER TWO

THE DISSOLUTION OF CAROLINGIAN UNITY

From Charlemagne to the Establishment of Feudalism (800-1000)

T he Carolingian dynasty, as we shall see, was short-lived. A variety of political factors eventually caused the breakup of this empire—with severe repercussions in both West and East. Out of this chaos emerged the intricate social structure we know as feudalism—the "glue" which held medieval society together. So let's pick up our story with Charlemagne and trace the developments from his reign through the rise and fall of feudalism.

WESTERN CHURCH AND EMPIRE TO THE MID-10TH CENTURY

Charlemagne—Holy Roman Emperor

The Emperor Charlemagne (742-814) is one of the most interesting persons in the entire Middle Ages. His biographer Einhard (770-840) leaves us many delightful details of the life of the first "Roman emperor" to rule in the West since the fifth century. According to Einhard, Charlemagne was seven feet tall, a pious and devout Christian, fascinated by learning and letters, and yet unable to master the skill of writing—even though he stored writing implements under his bed and tried mightily to learn. Einhard presents Charlemagne as something of a Renaissance man before the Renaissance.

According to Einhard, Charlemagne never really wanted to be an "emperor," and he regretted Pope Leo III's having transformed him from king of the Franks into Holy Roman Emperor in the year 800. Yet

Charlemagne was acutely aware of the parallels between his reign and the reign of the first Christian emperor, Constantine the Great. According to Einhard, Charlemagne's favorite book was Augustine's *City of God*, and Charlemagne no doubt thought of himself as the ideal emperor described by Augustine—a ruler whose every action was calculated to protect the Church and to encourage its ministry of salvation.

Charlemagne took seriously this sense of himself as protector of Church and faith. Even before he became emperor, while he was still king of the Franks, he expressed himself openly on the role which he saw himself called to play in salvation history:

> It is incumbent upon us, with God's help, to defend Holy Church outwardly with weapons everywhere against attacks by pagans and devastations by infidels, and *to consolidate her inwardly through the understanding of the true faith*. [Addressing the pope, he continued:] It is your task, Holy Father, like Moses to lift up your arms in prayer and go to aid our army...by your intercession.[1]

Notice how similar Charlemagne's conception of Church-State relations sounds to Constantine's. (See *The People of the Creed*, p. 19.) Both emperors looked upon themselves as the Church's protector and guide not only in external matters, but in internal and strictly theological matters as well. The supremacy of the papacy over the secular power which Pope Gregory the Great had established (see pp. 13, 15) was shattered by Charlemagne's insistence on serving as director-general of Church affairs. Thus the papacy once again fell under the dominion of the secular power, as in the days of Constantine and his sons.

Charlemagne's rule can accurately be considered a theocracy—that is, a government in which the king regards himself as divinely appointed and inspired to rule. This concept of government conformed exactly with the ancient Germanic notion of the tribal chieftain as both ruler and priest, a concept which obviously clashed with the popes' proclamation of themselves as "the supreme pontiffs." Yet, Pope Leo III (795-816), a man besieged by so many troubles in his own papal court, could hardly resist Charlemagne's theocratic tendencies.

Charlemagne saw himself obligated by God to restore the world to the ancient *Pax Romana*, and he interpreted this mandate to mean that all peoples should become Christian. But since the Roman idea of law and its universal peace was totally alien to the petty Germanic kings in the lands which Charlemagne sought to incorporate into his empire, he usually had to impose Christianity at the point of a sword.

After defeating a given tribe in battle, Charlemagne enforced a policy which can bluntly be described as "Be baptized or be killed!" Often entire tribes were simply lined up and swashed with holy water by Charlemagne's bishops, thus becoming "converts" to Christianity with little or no understanding of what was happening to them.

Yet Charlemagne was not so naive as to believe that such conversions made people devout Christians. He concentrated much of his time on defining and spreading Christian education. He appointed his own bishops and sent them to the far-flung regions of the empire (see map, p. 28) with instructions on how to evangelize his new subjects. He realized that the native priests ordained in these territories were abysmally ignorant of Christian doctrine, and thus he constantly tried to provide theological training for them. He also attempted to reform the moral laxity which existed everywhere among the native clergy.

The two principal vices of the clergy were simony and concubinage. Priests and bishops regularly bought and sold their offices, and everywhere both ranks of the clergy lived openly with mistresses or, in some cases, proudly carried on their duties while supporting large families. Frequently bishops would pass on both their office and its Church property to their sons, who either became bishops themselves or sold their inheritance for a handsome fee. In a theocratic empire, with Charlemagne conferring more and more power on his Frankish bishops, a bishopric or an abbey became a prized political plum.

Reform Under Emperor Louis

Everyone—emperor, pope and lower clergy—realized that the situation described above needed reform, but reform never made headway under Charlemagne, who was too occupied with empire-building. So the task of reform fell to Charlemagne's son Louis, who reigned as emperor from 814-840.

Louis's nickname was "the Pious," and for good reason. Whereas his father had been a man chiefly interested in science, mathematics, grammar and other fields of secular learning, Louis's chief interest was theology. He turned his attention from the bureaucratic machine his father had created and concentrated almost entirely on the reform of the Church. To organize his reform Louis divided his Christian subjects into three classes—canons, monks and laity.

The *canons* included bishops and secular priests (that is, not members of religious orders) affiliated with a particular church or parish. Groups of canons frequently lived together under the direction of a bishop near a cathedral church and came to be called "canons regular."

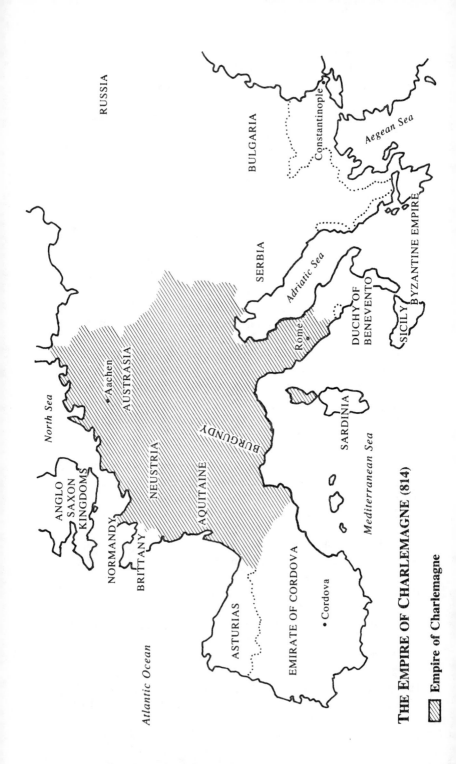

THE EMPIRE OF CHARLEMAGNE (814)

▨ **Empire of Charlemagne**

Monks were by and large still unordained during this period, but there was a growing number of monks who became priests. In many cases abbots rivaled bishops in power and authority because of the extensive lands under a monastery's control.

At the bottom of this pyramidal structure was the *laity*, who came to be looked upon less and less as Bede's priestly people (see p. 23) and more and more as the economic support group for the higher echelons.

From Louis's time on one is struck by the common prejudice in the West which viewed the laity as excluded from heaven. By the late Middle Ages it was commonly assumed that only priests and monks lived a life worthy of salvation. Berthold of Regensburg, for example, a popular 13th-century preacher, calculated the ratio of damned to saved as 100,000 to one.

Church-State Relations

Like Constantine centuries before (see *The People of the Creed*, p. 142), Emperor Louis imposed civil duties on his bishops. Thus it was often difficult to distinguish the imperial court from an episcopal synod. Louis felt that the key to Church reform lay in upgrading the education and morals of the parish priests, and thus he appointed his handpicked bishops to make regular visitations of parishes throughout the empire.

The reports of these civil-servant bishops did not encourage the Emperor: They found rampant illiteracy, concubinage, absenteeism and a profound sense of confusion as to what the priestly vocation entailed. Frequently the visiting bishop found parishes simply deserted by priests who had returned to a secular life-style apparently without even having thought that there was anything wrong in this.

Louis tried to remedy this situation by imposing minimum literacy standards upon priests and by providing for the upkeep of the clergy from the imperial treasury. All of this, of course, meant that the Church in Louis's empire was a state-controlled Church.

Louis did, however, look upon the Bishop of Rome differently than he did his local civil-servant bishops. For example, he promised not to interfere in papal elections, and he guaranteed papal autonomy within the Papal States. Louis's policy toward Rome coincided with two circumstances that were of immense significance for the future of Church-State relations in the West:

1) The Empire Unravels. In the first place, beginning about 828 the empire began to unravel as outlying regions seceded from imperial control. Hoping to stop the process of disintegration, Louis divided the empire in 839 among his four sons, thinking that decentralization of power would make for stronger control of the various parts of the empire. Eventually, three of Louis's sons—Lothair, Louis the German and Charles the Bald—divided the empire among themselves through the Treaty of Verdun (843).

Lothair was called "emperor," though the title meant nothing, and he ruled over northern Italy and portions of today's southern France; Louis the German became king of the East Franks and ruled what later came to be called Germany; Charles the Bald assumed control of the West Franks, roughly all the rest of France, ruling a people whose language was Romance rather than Germanic. From this threefold division, France, Germany, Italy and other European principalities would eventually emerge.

2) Three Strong Popes. The second significant development in Church-State relations after Charlemagne's death was the emergence of three strong popes: Nicholas I (858-867), Adrian II (867-872) and John VIII (872-882). Nicholas regained for the papacy much of the authority over Frankish bishops lost under Charlemagne and Louis the Pious. Nicholas, for example, refused to honor the divorce of Lothair's son, and he successfully resisted an imperial effort to gain control of the Papal States.

Further, Nicholas forced Hincmar, archbishop of the important Frankish see of Reims, to submit to papal control. Nicholas sent to Reims a "Vicar Apostolic for Germany and Gaul" who asserted the Pope's right to intervene in the affairs of Hincmar's diocese. Through such measures, Nicholas and the other ninth-century popes attempted to reassert the independence of the papacy from imperial domination and to reestablish their own authority over non-Italian bishops. Despite the limited success of the three popes named, Church-State relations in the West would nonetheless be marked by a constant struggle for supremacy waged by pope and emperor.

Further Disintegration of the Empire

The closing decades of the ninth century in the West were characterized by the further disintegration of the Carolingian Empire. Norsemen from Scandinavia steadily infiltrated the British Isles and northern France (giving the region its future name—"Normandy"). Moslems captured Sicily, Corsica and Sardinia, turning the Mediterranean into an Arab sea.

As the Carolingian Empire dissolved, autonomous barons emerged to assert control over various portions of the once unified Carolingian state. Robert, Count of Paris, for example, established himself and his heirs as rulers of a large territory in Northern France. This action culminated in the election in 987 of Robert's great-grandson, Hugh Capet, as the first king of France.

In the Frankish East, a family known as the Saxons managed to consolidate political power. In 936 the Saxon Otto I became king of what came to be known as Germany. Otto was crowned by Pope John XII as emperor in 962 and, as we shall see, promptly reasserted the empire's dominion over the papacy.

THE WESTERN CHURCH AND THE BYZANTINES

During the period discussed above the Eastern Church continued to be absorbed with the iconoclast controversy. (It had flared up again after Irene's death.) In addition, relations with the West worsened, both for political reasons—largely stemming from the West's new claim to imperial dignity—as well as for theological reasons.

The Final Defeat of Iconoclasm
What people pray is the most certain measure of what they believe: We saw this principle at work in the early period of Church history, and we see it at work again in the ultimate defeat of iconoclasm in the East. The iconoclasts were suspicious of the simple devotions of the faithful, while the defenders of icons saw in those devotions the very source of orthodoxy.

When the Byzantine bishops restored the use of icons once and for all in 843, they did so in the following terms:

> As the prophets have seen, as the apostles have taught, as the Church has received, as the theologians have taught, as the Church has agreed with one mind...so we believe, so we say, so we proclaim, honoring Christ, our true God and his saints, in our words, writings, ideas, sacrifices, temples and images.[2]

It was a magnificent statement of the Byzantine Church's effort to achieve wholeness—a wholeness that transcended time and space, binding together the ancient origins of Christian belief with the Church's present thinking, teaching and worship.

The Souring of East-West Relations
Although the iconoclast controversy ended in 843, peace did not return to Byzantine society. Intrigues and plots to overthrow this emperor and that patriarch were a constant fact of life in Constantinople. Two rival claimants to the patriarchal office, Ignatius and Photius, drove

the Byzantine Church into schism.

Pope Nicholas I, who as we have seen (p. 30) was eager to restore the papacy's claim to primacy in the West, also felt himself competent to intervene in the East. He thus "deposed" Photius and demanded the restoration of Ignatius as patriarch. The Byzantine Emperor Michael III wrote Nicholas a condescending letter in which he rejected the Pope's demands, pointing out that the pope was the emperor's subject, and not the other way around.

Photius, for his part, likewise condemned Pope Nicholas — but not just Nicholas. Photius declared the entire Western Church to be heretical because it had added the Latin word *filioque* ("and the Son") to the Creed of Constantinople in 381. That creed had stated that the Holy Spirit "proceeded from the Father" (see *The People of the Creed*, p. 79) and not from the Father *and* the Son. Photius was not above using this theological controversy to support his political ambitions, but it was true that the *filioque* was a bone in the throat of Byzantine theologians who regarded any tampering with the ancient creeds as heresy.

Other factors complicated the Western-Eastern situation. Pope Nicholas was greatly offended when Boris, king of the Bulgar tribes, decided to submit to the ecclesiastical jurisdiction of Constantinople rather than Rome. (The Bulgar tribes had accepted Christianity in 865 when Boris was baptized.) Thus did a large portion of the Slavic race enter the ranks of the Greek Church.

This process was facilitated by the invention of the Slavic alphabet by two brothers, Cyril and Methodius. Since the alphabet devised by these two missionaries was an adaptation of the Greek, Slavic nations such as Bulgaria, Serbia and Russia naturally gravitated toward Byzantine rather than Roman Christianity.

Theology and politics thus intertwined to make for a complex and explosive relationship between two entities that could no longer be considered two parts of the same Church but, rather, two distinct and separate Churches. The concept of a united Christendom was no longer viable after the demise of the Carolingians. We turn now to the one social force capable of holding medieval society together.

FEUDALISM — 'GLUE' OF MEDIEVAL SOCIETY

Feudalism was a means of organizing medieval society in which persons needing military protection bartered their labor for the security provided by an overlord. After the collapse of the Roman Empire people could no longer count on the Roman army for protection against marauding barbarians. Agricultural laborers in particular found themselves in grave peril because of the collapse of order, and thus they willingly surrendered themselves to the protection of the landed aristocracy who had the wealth to retain armed horsemen. These *knights*, as they came to be called, replaced the Roman foot soldier as feudal society's custodian of order.

The Structure of Feudalism

Between the years 600 and 1000 feudalism went through many changes, evolving into a very complex system of societal organization that differed from place to place. To get a highly generalized picture, we could think of classical feudalism in terms of a many-layered pyramid in which each level was subordinated to and owed certain duties to the next higher level. Let's analyze this model in more detail, beginning at the lowest level, the *slaves*.

As the Romans themselves had owned slaves so, too, did medieval Christians. Thomas Aquinas in the 13th century justified slavery by saying that it was a natural consequence of original sin. Gradually, however, as Christian landlords came to realize that the profit motive inspired people better than forced slavery, slaves increasingly won their freedom and entered into the rank of *serfs*.

Serfs were usually tenant farmers who were given the lifelong use of a portion of their lord's estate, called a *precarium*—which, because it could be terminated at will, was indeed precarious. In some places, however, serfs *owned* the land which they worked. Since the landlord usually granted the serf's plot of land to the serf's heirs when the latter died, serf families could be indentured to the same piece of land and to the same overlord's family for generations or even centuries.

Feudal society developed an extremely complex set of duties and responsibilities for the serf to perform. In most places the serf had to pay an annual head tax (so much money for everyone in his family), rent for use of the land and another tax levied annually at the whim of the landlord for no specific purpose whatever—perhaps simply for the right to exist as a serf. The landlord virtually owned the serf; in some places serfs could be sold. The landlord was thus literally the serf's lord (from "law-lord"); that is, he legally controlled every aspect of the serf's life.

The *peasants*, as serfs came to be called, made up the vast majority of the European population—well over 90 percent in most areas. They knew their place in society and rarely left it—at least until the 14th century, as we shall see later. The lords looked upon the peasants as little more than cattle. One lord noted that his peasants had the mentality of sheep and no fear of God in their hearts. Yet the peasants and their lord lived closely together in a fixed and indissoluble unit on the lord's *manor*, which was an agricultural commune or small village where a given lord and his serfs resided.

Directly above the serf in the feudal pyramid stood the least powerful *freeman* who owned land and controlled serfs. To his serfs this freeman was a lord, but to his own immediate lord he was a *vassal*. The responsibilities of the lord were to provide security for his vassals, supervise and administer agricultural productivity on his estate and serve his own *liege lord* (or immediate overlord) as a soldier when asked to do so.

The land which a vassal held under his liege lord was called a *fief*. Liege lords, although absolute masters of their vassals' destiny, were nonetheless required to protect and befriend their vassals. If they did not, vassals could *defief* ("de-fy") their lords and remove themselves from *fealty*. This complex web of interrelationships between various ranks of lords and vassals is called *subinfeudation*.

Feudalism naturally suited the interests of the Catholic Church, which had already achieved its own pyramidal structure (see *The People of the Creed*, p. 139). Further, since the Church between 600 and 1000 came to be the largest landowner in Europe, *bishops* and *abbots* served as powerful lords in the feudal system. The Benedictine monastery of Fulda in Germany, for example, owned enough land to maintain 15,000 manors; the bishop of Tours in France lorded it over 20,000 serfs.

Bishops and abbots acquired purely secular titles such as duke or count, minted their own coin, judged civil lawsuits and rode about dressed in armor as they went off to war like any other lord. By the 11th century no one in medieval Europe knew a bishop or an abbot who was not also a powerful secular lord.

At the apex of the feudal pyramid stood the *king*. Until the 12th century the kings of Europe were simply the most powerful landlords, but they were anything but absolute monarchs. They owed their election as king (or their winning of the office in war) to their vassals, and the latter took pains to make the king acutely aware that he could not safely abuse his power.

Further, although the fief of the king was theoretically the entire state (conferred on him by God, it was believed), kings actually controlled much less land than did the Church. Monarchy in the early Middle Ages was, therefore, a very tenuous privilege. Gradually, as Christian society became more feminized by the growth of contemplative spirituality, *queens* were allowed to rule in the absence of a king.

The Military Society

All through the Middle Ages war was a staple of life. Feudalism itself owed its birth to the dissolution of order and the resulting need for military protection. Every feudal lord was a soldier, and the entire feudal pyramid was little more than a military heirarchy: princes, dukes, counts and archbishops served as generals; barons, bishops and abbots were lower-grade officers; knights led platoons of serfs.

Even when lords or kings from different regions were not fighting each other, rival dukes, counts and barons from the same region (many of whom were also bishops) often waged private war. Such conflicts were looked upon not so much as war but as sport. To the lords the death of a few dozen serfs or a knight or two didn't matter; what was important was the respect one gained in besting one's rival and earning a reputation for bravery. Feudal war was the football game of the Middle Ages.

Since the Roman infantry's defeat at Adrianople in 378 (see *The People of the Creed*, p. 114), horse soldiers had replaced infantry as the most effective means of killing and maiming. The Middle Ages continued the trend toward cavalry, giving birth to the entire code of military conduct known as *chivalry*, from the French word for horse, *cheval* (from which *cavalier* and *chevalier* are also derived).

By the code of chivalry a noble captive in a war was to be released on his oath not to take up arms again in the same conflict and to send a ransom back to his former captors after being released. King Louis IX obeyed this code to a fault; his Moslem captors in the Eighth Crusade demanded a ransom totaling more than the crown's entire annual income. Yet, upon returning home, Louis taxed his subjects to raise the ransom and then shipped it east.

When the soldiers of King Edward I of England (1272-1307) became adept in the use of the longbow, chivalry began to decline for the simple reason that Edward's bowmen shot opposing knights' horses out from under them. To this development add cannon and gunpower in the 14th century and one arrives at the collapse of chivalry.

On the whole, medieval war was not anywhere near as brutal or as horrible as modern war. Only a small percentage of warriors were killed. At the Battle of Bouvines in 1214, for example—a major conflict involving England, France, Germany and the papacy—1,500 knights fought but only 170 were killed.

Despite such statistics, however, feudal war exacted a terrible toll on the peasantry. It was *their* tilled land that was torn up, their houses that were razed, their daughters who were raped (chivalric civility did not apply to serfs) and their livestock which was stolen for food.

In addition, independent mercenary knights, not tied to any lord, roamed about stealing and murdering at will. A Galahad or Lancelot courageously protecting the weak and defenseless was the exception rather than the rule.

The Church finally intervened to protect the unarmed peasant. Beginning in the late 10th century, various Church councils ordered marauding knights not to harm unarmed peasants and enforced the decree with the threat of excommunication. The Church's ban came to be known as the "Peace of God."

With a similar declaration known as the "Truce of God," the Church specified certain days and times when all fighting must cease. Eventually the Church allotted only 80 days each year to private warfare. As this custom took hold, private warfare virtually ceased, especially as the rise of nation-states siphoned off the best knights for more deadly national conflicts, of which The Hundred Years' War is the best example (see pp. 147-150).

The Decline of Feudalism

When a strong merchant/urban class began to develop in the 11th century, kings began to liberate themselves from the control of their baronial vassals. In the new city-dwelling merchants the kings found willing allies for the cause of centralization vis-à-vis feudal particularism. By the year 1200, feudalism was being threatened by new social forces: the growth of cities, the rebirth of commerce and industry, capitalism, the development of universities, animosity between the classes, and the influx of Arabic and Greek culture and learning following the Crusades.

Only the Church continued to maintain a purely feudal organization as the rest of European society began to coalesce around strong central governments. As these governments gained strength they could no longer abide the autonomy of the last bastion of feudalism—the Church—nor could they tolerate the Church's political power.

As long as feudalism prevailed the Church had a role to play in preserving social stability; as feudalism declined, however, centralized monarchies superseded the Church as the preserver of order. To the new monarchies of the high Middle Ages, the Church slowly came to be seen as the enemy of social progress.

Before progressing any further with the historical events of the Middle Ages, let us spend a chapter discussing theological trends during feudalism's golden age.

CHAPTER THREE

DOCTRINE AND DEVOTION STRIVE FOR WHOLENESS

Western Theology and Spirituality Before Scholasticism

Beginning in the ninth century, Western theologians slowly began to move beyond the blind acceptance of past tradition and to develop their own theology. They began to make new and innovative interpretations of what Augustine and the other Fathers had said. This rereading of the Fathers was seen by some traditionalists, however, as a threat to orthodoxy.

CHALLENGES TO ORTHODOXY

Archbishop Hincmar of Reims said that those who took new approaches to the traditional doctrine were "stirring up idle chatter in opposition to the true faith."[1] Another writer characterized the new look at dogma as the work of the devil, who was "attempting to undermine the fortified walls of the faith."[2] And an even more pessimistic observer stated that "the study of doctrine, by which faith and the knowledge of God ought to be nourished and to grow day by day, is extinct almost everywhere."[3]

Such gloomy remarks were clearly exaggerations. The Augustinian tradition was hardly in peril. Ninth-century theologians weren't trying to overthrow tradition or to destroy orthodoxy; they were simply thinking for themselves and asking original questions about the faith. Some theologians did, however, venture into areas which the Church could not accept as orthodox. Let's take a brief look at some of these controversial new teachings.

The Adoptionist Controversy

In the fourth century certain bishops erroneously taught that Jesus at some point in his life had been "adopted" by the Father (see *The People of the Creed*, p. 45). What these bishops meant was that Jesus was an ordinary man who, at some point in his life such as his baptism in the Jordan, became "possessed" of the Father's divinity. An offshoot of this adoptionist thinking cropped up in Spain during the early part of Charlemagne's reign.

The two leading Spanish adoptionists were Archbishop Elipandus of Toledo (718-802) and Bishop Felix of Urgel (d. 818). Neither Elipandus nor Felix were adoptionists in the strict fourth-century sense. They believed that Jesus was fully Son of God, yet they did distinguish between Jesus as Son of God and Jesus as Son of Man.

According to Felix, when the Church taught that the Son of Man and the Son of God were one and the same person, what it really was saying was that the Father—through grace—had "adopted" the Son of Man (Jesus' human nature) by bestowing on him the divinity and title of Son of God (Jesus' divine nature). Expanding this idea, Elipandus wrote that, while Jesus was God's only-begotten son by nature, he was yet the "first-born of many brothers" (Romans 8:29) only by adoption and not by nature. The fallacy of the two bishops' position was to make Jesus of Nazareth similar to every other human being except for the miracle of the Father's adoption of him as Son of God.

This position was contrary to Augustine's teaching that Jesus had been God's only-begotten son not only in his divinity but also in his humanity. Thus, for Augustine, Jesus—although fully human—was nonetheless the Father's son by nature and not by grace. As Charlemagne's court tutor Alcuin of York characterized the "Spanish error": "If Christ were Son of God by nature but yet adopted by the Father, he is simultaneously one person and another person."[4]

The adoptionist position would have shattered the Christological formula from the Council of Chalcedon (451)—"one person in two natures"—by substituting something like "two persons transformed by the Father into one nature." Archbishop Hincmar of Reims attacked this error when he wrote, "There are not two Christs, nor two Sons, but one Christ, one Son, both God and man, because God, the Son of God, assumed a human nature, not a human person."[5] Spanish Adoptionism was condemned at the Synod of Frankfurt in 794.

The Trinitarian Dispute

Another divergence from the traditional interpretation of Augustine's doctrine was the trinitarian teaching of a German

Benedictine monk, Gottschalk, who about the year 830 emigrated to the French monastery of Orbais. Gottschalk used a troubling phrase, "Trine [not triune] *deity,*" to refer to the Trinity, saying that "each person of the Trinity has its own deity and divinity."[6] Thus, according to Gottschalk, only the Son among the three persons assumed a human nature. A quick glance at Augustine's trinitarian theology as discussed in *The People of the Creed* (p. 125) illustrates how Gottschalk's trinitarian theology clashed with Augustine's.

Hincmar of Reims once again defended the traditional Augustinian view by condemning Gottschalk as a tritheist (one who believes in three gods). Like Augustine, Hincmar taught "a single and identical action of the Trinity,"[7] so that the entire Trinity could be said to have participated in the Incarnation, not just the second person of the Trinity. Gottschalk's position was condemned at the Synod of Soissons in 853.

The interesting feature of both the adoptionist and trinitarian debates is that both sides to each debate appealed to Augustine as support for their positions. Bishop Elipandus, for example, quoted a passage from Augustine's mentor, Ambrose, who had called Christ "an adoptive son," and Gottschalk pointed to Augustine's use of "trine unity" as support for his own trinitarian position. Hincmar's claim, therefore, that Gottschalk "invented new and unheard of things, which are contrary to the ancient understanding of the orthodox,"[8] did not ring entirely true. Further, Hilary of Poitiers (315-367; see *The People of the Creed*, p. 108) was discovered to have talked about Christ's flesh as having been "adopted."

Thus, although the Spanish adoptionist doctrine and Gottschalk's trinitarian views were condemned, theologians began to feel less certain than before that the ancient Fathers had all taught the same unambiguous doctrine.

The Reemergence of Predestination

During this period of reexamining patristic doctrine, Augustine's most provocative teaching—predestination—came under close theological scrutiny. Again it was Gottschalk who questioned Augustinian orthodoxy and Hincmar who defended it. And once again both men quoted Augustine to support their mutually exclusive positions.

Why was predestination such an important issue? In an age when chaos and instability predominated over law and order, theologians tended to emphasize doctrines that would explain the general state of immorality. Predestination, by positing that many people were predestined to reprobation and evil, was one of these doctrines. In the doctrine of predestination the Middle Ages anticipated by seven centuries one of the major issues of the Reformation.

Gottschalk's theory of "double predestination" was based on his belief in God's unalterable will. According to Gottschalk, God cannot change his mind, otherwise he would be changeable like his creation. Thus God had to have foreordained both the salvation of the elect and the damnation of the wicked. As Gottschalk explained it, "If God does something that he has not done by predestination, he will simply have to change,"[9] which for Gottschalk was an impossibility. Gottschalk, of course, was able to find Augustinian language to support his position.

Hincmar challenged Gottschalk on the very point that had led to the solution achieved by the Synod of Orange (529), namely, the distinction between predestination and God's foreknowledge. (See *The People of the Creed*, p. 135.)

Hincmar concluded that, while Christ offered salvation to all, "not all are redeemed by the mystery of his suffering."[10] Gottschalk, on the other hand, said that Christ died only for those who were predestined to be saved. Thus, Hincmar taught that salvation was available to all though not all accepted it, while Gottschalk essentially merged the concepts of salvation and redemption by saying that Christ had died only for the elect and that only they were redeemed. The Council of Quiercy in 853 supported Hincmar's position and condemned Gottschalk's.

The Conflict Over the Eucharist

Radbertus (790-865), a Benedictine monk from the north of France, initiated a debate on the Eucharist when he criticized "certain brethren" who were reluctant to assert Jesus' Real Presence in the Eucharist. The chief "brethren" Radbertus had in mind was a fellow Benedictine named Ratramnus (d. 868).

For Radbertus the bread of the Eucharist was entirely identical to the historical Jesus. Ratramnus, on the other hand, argued that Radbertus's position was logically inconsistent with history: Jesus could not have turned bread and wine into his body and blood while he was still seated in front of his disciples. Otherwise, Ratramnus said, there would have been two different persons known as Jesus—one a man with arms and legs and the other someone miraculously hidden in a loaf of bread.

Radbertus, however, was undeterred. He elaborated upon his Eucharistic theory by saying that once the words of consecration were spoken, what looked like bread and wine was really only the "figure" of bread and wine. In reality this "figure" was "nothing other than the flesh and blood of Christ."[11] For Radbertus, a double miracle took place at the consecration: (1) Bread and wine were changed into Christ's body and blood, even though (2) the bread and wine continued to look and taste like bread and wine.

Ratramnus disagreed with Radbertus's interpretation. For him, after the words of consecration were spoken, the bread and wine remained bread and wine, but through the faith of the believer they were permeated, as it were, with Christ's presence. For Ratramnus, then, the consecrated host was not Jesus' "real flesh" but "the *sacrament* of the real flesh."[12]

Ratramnus quoted Augustine to support his position. Augustine, who actually was rather ambiguous on the Real Presence, had often talked about the "Body of Christ" as a synonym for the worshiping community, and he had compared the "eating" of Jesus' flesh to an act of faith in Jesus. As Ratramnus read Augustine, the Eucharist was principally a spiritual reality.

Radbertus, too, cited Augustine, as well as Augustine's spiritual master, Ambrose, who had relied for his own Eucharistic theology on the prayers of the Mass. As Radbertus read the canon of the Mass, it appeared unequivocal to him that "after the consecration the true flesh and blood of Christ is truly *believed* to be present."[13] Radbertus, then, relied ultimately on the liturgy to support his position, and for that reason Radbertus's position came to be accepted over Ratramnus's. Once again, what Christians prayed determined what they believed.

ERIGENA: A BREATH OF FRESH AIR

In contrast to Radbertus and Ratramnus, who relied almost exclusively on the Fathers, John Scotus Erigena was a truly original and creative thinker—the first in the Middle Ages.

Erigena (810-877) was a man ahead of his times, a thinker thoroughly steeped in classical philosophy and a proponent of the use of reason to support the truths of revelation. He was an Irishman who thought like a Greek; he was as familiar with Eastern theologians like Pseudo-Dionysius, Gregory of Nyssa and Maximus the Confessor as he was with Augustine.

Erigena did not look over his shoulder as did the other theologians of his day; he felt confident to draw his own conclusions without first paying tribute to the Fathers. His purpose was not to fit theology into "the walls of the Catholic faith," as his predecessors had attempted to do. Rather, as he himself put it, he wrote for those "who demand from Catholics a rational account of the Christian religion."[14]

Erigena was an adventurer; he was willing to allow human reason to roam free as it speculated about theological issues. It was this tendency which drew down upon him the accusations of many detractors. Erigena believed that true philosophy and true religion could not contradict each other. For him, all truth was one, whether arrived at through reason or believed in faith. He thus anticipated Thomas Aquinas by four centuries.

The Introduction of Dialectic

Erigena applied the ancient Greek philosophical method known as *dialectic* to medieval theology. He called this method "the mother of the arts."[15] Later Western theologians would use his method to construct their great syntheses.

Dialectic concerned itself with the science of correct reasoning. We would simply equate dialectic with our word *logic*. It was a method of argumentation by syllogism, that is, proposing two premises and a conclusion: "All humans are mortal. Mary is a human. Mary is a mortal." Eventually it evolved into a system of argumentation in which a thesis is contrasted by an antithesis and a new synthesis is proposed. (Dialectic was one of the seven liberal arts introduced into Western education at Charlemagne's court by Alcuin of York.) After Erigena's death it would be the means by which a new way of thinking known as Scholasticism began to develop.

For Erigena, dialectic was God's gift and should be used to glorify the Creater. Through dialectic one started with faith and ascended to "theological reason," by which Erigena meant a higher spiritual understanding of doctrine.

Erigena's Byzantine Orientation

Similar to Byzantine thinkers, Erigena said nature could be divided into that which is and that which is not. Erigena defined that which is not as that which is beyond the senses and thus beyond the power of the mind to grasp. By this definition what is not can be called *essence*, while what is—what can be sensed—can be defined as *accident*. Since God was beyond all accidents (time, space, color, etc.) one could really say only what God is not, not what he is.

Here, of course, Erigena relied heavily on the apophatic theology developed by Pseudo-Dionysius and Maximus the Confessor (see pp. 21-22). Since God was pure essence (pure spirit), it would be correct to say of him that he is "nothing." Erigena explained this as a nothingness which encompasses everything, by going beyond everything we can imagine. God, then, is "superessential," beyond even essence itself. We predicate essence of God only because we conceive of transcendent reality in this way; but God in himself, as he really is, is beyond the limitation of words such as "essence."

Yet the great beauty of the Christian revelation for Erigena is that this superessential mystery who we name God is at the same time utterly present to his creation. As Erigena stated it, "All things are in God, since he himself *is* all things.[16] This did not make Erigena a pantheist. When Erigena says God *is* all things, he means something which our language cannot express. He means that God "*be's*" us, that he constantly loves us into being. God is *is-ness* and thus we *are*. That which is cannot be separate from that which "*be's*" it, but it is not identical to it. God, in this sense, *is* the creature, but the creature is not God.

The source of our individual humanity, our creaturely sense of individuality, Erigena said, is the eternal *Logos*, the Word of God (John 1:1). Within the Word, from all eternity, we existed as "forms" in the mind of God, as potential manifestations of being yet unactualized. (Erigena, like Augustine, was a Neoplatonist; see *The People of the Creed*, p. 125.) At the moment of our conception we begin to exist in ourselves, whereas previously we had only existed "causally" within the divine Word, whom Erigena called "the form of forms." Erigena's critics accused him of emanationism — that is, the belief in God's emanation into lesser grades of being rather than in God's creation of such beings.

GRACE, NATURE AND PREDESTINATION

Erigena denied such charges of emanationism. For him there was not such a drastic separation between "grace" and "nature" as there was for the other theologians of his day. Erigena simply equated "the gifts of divine grace" with "all the good things that are distributed to us in this life."[17]

This greatly troubled his critics, who posited an essential dichotomy between grace and nature. Radbertus, for example, placed the Eucharist and Mary's virginity into the realm of grace, declaring that nature had no part to play in such divine mysteries. This type of thinking, however, struck Erigena as narrow.

To Erigena, arguing about such things as predestination detracted from God's goodness, as if God's creation could somehow be lost to him. For Erigena God's being and willing were equivalent. Thus, God could not will damnation for that which shared in his own being. Indeed, Erigena believed, as Origen had, in the universal restoration of all things in Christ based on his interpretation of 1 Corinthians 15:28. Eventually,

43

Erigena believed, Christ would be "all in all" as Paul had written; eventually all of God's creation would return to God in glorified form. Thus, for Erigena to speak of predestination meant only predestination to salvation and to deification.

Such thoughts scandalized other ninth-century theologians, who called Erigena "a master of error." Florus of Lyons said that Erigena's chief error was to base his thought on "human, and as he himself boasts, philosophical arguments."[18] The Church was not yet ready to tolerate a synthesis between faith and reason. Portions of Erigena's writings were officially condemned, but not until the 13th century. Perhaps it took four centuries for Church officials to know what to make of a man who defined theology as "a kind of poetry" and who believed that nature in its goodness would live forever.

However Erigena was later judged, he was a remarkable phenomenon for his day, a man who opened up the windows of the stuffy chamber of ninth-century theology and allowed in a fresh breeze. It was a breeze that would continue to circulate for centuries.

THE BEGINNING OF WESTERN MARIOLOGY

As in the East, Western Mariology (study of Mary) developed largely out of the liturgy. In other words, Western Christians were expressing devotion to Mary in their communal prayer life well before theologians worked out the details of Marian doctrine. Once again, the prayers of the faithful helped determine the direction of Christian thinking.

We find the beginnings of Mariology in Marian prayers, such as the one written by Archbishop Ildefonsus of Toledo (607-667): "I pray thee, I pray thee, O Holy Virgin, that I may have Jesus by the same Spirit by whom thou didst give birth to Jesus."[19] Another theologian urged prayers to Mary because, as he put it, "We cannot find anyone more powerful in merits than she is for placating the wrath of the judge, she who did merit to become the mother of the Redeemer and judge."[20]

Here we see three ideas which were to become typical of later medieval Marian thinking: (1) prayers may be addressed directly to Mary; (2) Mary is the most "merit-filled" of all the saints; and (3) she acts as a mediator between sinful humanity and God, the fearsome "judge."

Ninth-century Christians were acutely aware of God's wrath since they believed it was manifested all around them in the chaos and brutality of their everyday lives. In the popular imagination it was easy to equate the harshness of everyday life—the cruelty of feudal warfare and the menial servitude of the peasants—with the punishment sent by the wrathful God of the Old Testament. Most Christians saw a direct relationship between one's lowly status in feudal society and one's sinfulness.

The continued concern with predestination, and the generally-held assumption that the lower-class laity constituted the majority of those denied salvation, contributed to a mass projection of negativism onto the angry Old Testament male deity. Jesus, too, came to be seen more and more as a stern and angry judge—consider, for example, the fierce *pantokrator* of Byzantine iconography. Church art of this period depicted almost exclusively scenes of the Last Judgment and hell; very rarely does one find scenes reminiscent of heaven or eternal happiness.

Out of this environment it was only natural for Christians to seek a softer, more approachable intermediary between themselves and God. In the popular imagination Mary became this intermediary. Although no Christian writer of the period ascribed divinity to Mary, by conceiving of her as a "mediatrix" between humanity and God, most Christians subconsciously attributed to Mary feminine qualities of God.

Developments in Mariology naturally led to the question of whether Mary had required salvation in the same way as other human beings had. One answer to this question was given by Radbertus, who taught that, although Mary had been conceived in sin like everyone else, she was yet "not subject to any transgressions when she was born and did not contract original sin in the sanctified womb."[21]

Notice two things about Radbertus's statement: (1) it is not a belief in immaculate conception since it places Mary's liberation from original sin "in the sanctified womb"; thus, (2) it does not deviate from Augustine's doctrine of original sin as humanity's "hereditary disease" passing to each new human embryo at the moment of conception. Future theologians would question Radbertus's position, arguing that one could deduce Mary's freedom from original sin only by saying that she was *conceived* immaculate; that is, that she was *never* subject to original sin.

Ninth-century theologians also speculated about the ancient belief in Mary's bodily assumption. Here theologians were not innovative; it was enough for them that the Assumption was a genuine feast of the Church (see *The People of the Creed*, p. 144). The general position concerning Mary's assumption was that taken by Abbot Ambrose Autpert, who wrote: "The correct position regarding her assumption is shown to be this, that—without knowing 'whether in the body or out of the body,' as the apostle says—we believe that she was

45

assumed higher than the angels."[22]

Western Spirituality to the Mid-10th Century

The reform of Louis the Pious (see pp. 27,29) affected not only external Church organization and policy, but also the everyday lives of believers. Everywhere ninth-century preachers called for a true conversion to Christ and the gospel. Bishops and priests exhorted secular rulers to become ministers of God for the salvation of the laity. The concept of the Christian prince who not only managed temporal affairs, but who also directed the spiritual well-being of his subjects became an ideal that was constantly advanced in spiritual literature and preaching, though never actually achieved.

Canons and Monks

Beginning with Emperor Louis the Pious, the distinction between canons, monks and laity became an increasingly more rigid standard. It was thought that each rank within Christian society should have its own spirituality. Early spiritual writers would never have conceived of a unified spirituality for all three classes.

For the canons, or "regular clergy," Bishop Chrodegang of Metz composed a "canonical order" by which he sought to regulate the spiritual life of those in the first rank. Chrodegang's "order" evolved into a "Rule" which became something of a general pattern for the spiritual instruction of the regular clergy throughout Western Europe. The Rule stressed shared liturgical life, promoted communal living wherever possible and expressed the hope that the clergy would live a life of poverty. Louis the Pious was so impressed by the Rule that he tried to implement it throughout the empire, but never really succeeded.

The writings directed toward the regular clergy, such as Chrodegang's Rule, lacked one ingredient which monks regarded as essential: the development of the Christian's interior life through contemplative prayer. All spiritual literature directed to the regular clergy defined prayer as *liturgical* prayer—that is, the "Divine Office" which was to be chanted or recited in common. Further, since the regular clergy received the same training in the liberal arts as did the sons of princes in the Carolingian schools, canonical spirituality was largely centered in the intellect rather than in the heart.

A greater dignity was generally accorded to the regular clergy in comparison to the monks. Yet monastic spirituality was nonetheless considered superior to that of the regular clergy, since it was based on evangelical poverty and the inner transformation of the soul through constant meditation on Scripture and through contemplative prayer.

Consequently, it was the Monastic Rule of St. Benedict which became during the eighth and ninth centuries the source of the deepest level of Christian spirituality. Everywhere Benedictine houses—emptied by the invasions and chaos of the previous two centuries—were rebuilt and filled with novices, and new foundations were established. Monasteries in Carolingian times were called "holy cities" where, it was believed, Christians could come close to living the life of heaven on earth.

In these "holy cities" the virtues of poverty, chastity and obedience were the means by which the monk rose to the higher states of spiritual life, characterized by Abbot Ambrose Autpert of the monastery of St. Vincent in southern Italy as "the Sabbath calm." The Sabbath calm was a state of "spiritual leisure" which made it possible for the monk to experience within his own consciousness the mysteries of Jesus' life, and through "the gift of tears" to recapitulate the sufferings of Jesus.

Monks during this period had little of the intellectual training of the regular clergy; their spirituality was based on the heart rather than the intellect. Not until later centuries would monasteries become great centers of study and learning. Still, the monks of the ninth century were educated enough to make exquisite copies of the Bible and patristic writings.

The Benedictine Contribution

One of the most important commentators on monastic spirituality was Benedict of Aniane (750-821), abbot of a great monastery in southeastern France which he had founded on his own property. Benedict of Aniane reorganized the Benedictine Order as no one before him, and both Charlemagne and Louis the Pious urged him to spread his system of Benedictine discipline to other monasteries of the empire. Benedict of Aniane greatly increased the liturgical practice of his monks so that the better part of their day was spent in choir chanting the psalter.

At the same time he emphasized the centrality of *lectio divina*—the "divine reading" of Scripture—in the life of each monk. For Benedict, *lectio* was the gateway to the contemplative life. He defined a spiritual methodology in which the monk started each period of his day with common prayers, followed by private reading of Scripture (*lectio*), meditation upon the passage read (*meditatio*) and, finally, contemplation (*contemplatio*), which Benedict described as a state in which the monk passes "from faith to sight." Benedict's three-stage program of *lectio*, *meditatio* and *contemplatio* was to become the standard monastic spiritual method throughout the Middle Ages.

Another dimension to Benedictine spirituality was advanced by the ninth-century monk Hildemar in his *Commentary* on the Rule of St. Benedict (the *first* St. Benedict; see *The People of the Creed*, p. 148). Hildemar described the conditions under which a monk could choose, with the consent of his abbot, to leave the community and live the life of a hermit. Hildemar described the hermit's life as a "greater good" than life in the cloister, thus foreshadowing the rise of the hermitic movements of later centuries. Hildemar stressed that monastic life is above all a life of deep personal intimacy with Jesus Christ.

Deviating from Benedict of Aniane's emphasis on liturgical prayer, Hildemar stressed the importance of manual labor performed in silence and in recollection on the Scriptures. Such labor, Hildemar said, leads to the gift of tears and to contemplation. Hildemar was suspicious of long periods of silent prayer, which he characterized as "Greek prayer." For Hildemar, obedience to the Rule, *lectio* and manual labor were the basis of contemplation. Long periods of mystical union were not to be sought; they were enitrely gifts of grace when and if they appeared at all.

By comparing Benedict of Aniane's writings with Hildemar's, we notice a dichotomy in monastic spirituality which was to become more and more significant in later years. Whereas Benedict of Aniane developed a methodology of prayer, Hildemar saw prayer as a more spontaneous process flowing naturally from the ordinary practice of obedience and from manual labor. This tension between "willed" and "graced" contemplation—something not consciously addressed by either Benedict or Hildemar—was to become of great significance to later spirituality, both in West and East.

Lay Spirituality

Bishop Jonas of Orleans (d. 844) noticed that, while much had been written on spiritual instruction for monks and canons, little was available for the laity. Jonas thus composed spiritual treatises directed toward the laity, and a general trend in this direction gradually developed. Since to spiritual writers "the laity" meant "the laity who could read," and since the lower classes were largely illiterate, these treatises were of necessity directed to the nobility. Hincmar of Reims, for example, wrote a book entitled *On the Person and Ministry of a King* in which he exhorted princes to instruct the common people in Christian morality.

Jonas of Orleans urged princes to search their consciences daily and to repent often of any sin found there. "Erase your sins with tears," he urged. He criticized the simple folk for not receiving Communion more often and admonished them to prepare themselves by repentance and confession of sins.

In the ninth century the idea of the Mass as a sacrifice had gradually become as important as belief in the Real Presence of Jesus in the bread and wine. As a result, Christians were exhorted to attend the sacrifice of the Mass even if they did not receive Communion, as if the two actions were separate and distinct. Attendance at the sacrifice gradually became more and more the motive for attendance at Mass, and thus not only the consecration but also the reception of the bread and wine increasingly became solely the priest's affair.

Along with the admonition to frequent Communion, Jonas also urged those who could do so to read the Scriptures daily. To assist the laity in this task Jonas and other spiritual writers composed abbreviated sections from the Bible, which came to be known as *breviaries*. Bishop Prudentius of Troyes (d. 861), for example, wrote *A Breviary of the Psalter* to assist a certain noblewoman to remain faithful to daily Bible study while she traveled.

Though theoretically directed by virtuous princes, lay spirituality was in actuality affected more by monasticism than by princes — few of whom attained to virtue. As ninth-century Europe began to regain its agricultural foundation, small villages clustered around the monks, who themselves became masters of farming. There was frequent contact between lay folks and monks, no matter how greatly monasticism stressed the ideal of solitude and separation from the world.

While the regular clergy in the towns sequestered themselves from the lower classes, the monks and country peasants, who were frequently of the same stock, rubbed shoulders with each other. An intermediate type of monastic calling soon developed — the "lay brotherhood." These men lived within the cloister but performed manual labor *without* attending to the liturgical duties of the "choir monks." The spirituality of these lay brothers spread back into the farms and villages and acted as a link communicating monastic spirituality to the lower classes of the laity.

We see the influence of monasticism on lay spirituality in the way discipline and asceticism gradually developed as an ideal for *all* Christians. The writings of Rabanus Maurus (776-856), abbot of Fulda in Germany and later Archbishop of Mainz, greatly affected both monastic and lay spirituality. Rabanus wrote treatises on "Christian warfare," by which he meant a kind of psychological struggle for the soul waged between God and the devil.

Rabanus's concern was with interior repentance and inner conversion. He focused on the heavenly reward which awaited those who through asceticism, prayer and good works achieved a "hidden martyrdom" which led them to salvation. Christian spirituality came to be seen as a struggle to reform every aspect of one's life by submitting to the demands of the gospel.

The Role of the Bible

Everywhere the Bible was held up as the source of sanctity. There is no more egregious falsehood than the myth which characterizes the Catholic Middle Ages as a time in which the Bible was hidden from the laity. On the contrary, the Church made great efforts to spread the Bible to every corner of the Carolingian empire, but this was no easy task. Charlemagne, for example, lamented the paucity and poor quality of the Bibles which he had at his disposal. There was the further problem of almost universal illiteracy in Latin, the only language in which the Scriptures had been preserved from antiquity.

The task of copying the Sacred Scriptures fell largely to the monks. As the monks copied the ancient manuscripts, they turned their finished products into priceless art treasures, adorning them with magnificent calligraphy, sketches and goldwork. This process of copying took time, and there were few who could either afford or read what the monks' hands produced. For these practical reasons, and not because of a clerical conspiracy to keep the laity ignorant of God's Word, Bibles were seldom owned or read by the laity.

Yet the core of lay spirituality was biblical nonetheless. "The Bible" for the average Christian became the oral Bible, which he or she heard preached during liturgies, and the graphic Bible, which was painted on the walls of churches and stitched into tapestries.

The biblical foundation of lay spirituality is seen particularly in the Carolingian adaptation of the Roman liturgy. From the eighth century onward the Frankish kings adhered to the Roman canon of the Mass. Yet the Franks added to the Roman canon their own folk piety, hymns and devotions. In these additions many biblical themes are stressed, particularly the idea of Christ as king and as universal victor over evil. Marian devotion also became very popular.

Doctrine or Devotion: Which Comes First?

Let us summarize our pre-Scholastic contact with Western theology and spirituality by observing how difficult it is to determine whether theology influenced spirituality or spirituality influenced theology. Doctrine and devotion grew side by side in the early medieval

West. Theology dared not extend itself beyond the faith of the ordinary believer as symbolized in the Christian's everyday worship. At the same time the ordinary believer was constantly influenced by the work of theologians in ways the ordinary believer did not realize.

Together theology and spirituality attempted to recapture the wholeness of thought and faith which the ninth-century Christian believed to have characterized the life of the early Church. Gradually, however, the lure of the past diminished and medieval Christians began to extend the horizons of their quest for wholeness beyond the boundaries of antiquity and into new realms of thought and faith.

CHAPTER FOUR

THE RESURGENCE OF PAPAL AUTHORITY

From Otto I to the Concordat of Worms (962-1122)

We begin this chapter with the Western institutional Church in a state of submission to a new emperor (the German King Otto I) and end with the papacy on the verge of establishing a unified, supranational Church. In order to see how such a dramatic change occurred, the many events of medieval Church history from 962-1122 are here compressed into a generalized account.

EMPEROR VS. POPE: VYING FOR CHURCH CONTROL

When Pope John XII crowned Otto I Holy Roman Emperor in 962 (see map, p. 54), he initiated a tradition in which German kings were to occupy this Western imperial office until 1918.

Otto I surpassed even Charlemagne in his attempts to intervene in Church affairs. Otto saw himself as the protector of the papacy and the director of the Church. He increased the size of the Papal States by granting the popes lands amounting to nearly two-thirds of the Italian peninsula. But he made it clear in doing so that it was he and not the pope who was the true sovereign of these territories.

In 963, when Pope John XII conspired with Italian nobles to rid himself of Otto's suzerainty, the emperor and his troops went to Rome and regained control, forcing the Roman nobility to agree never to elect another pope without imperial approval. Otto then deposed John XII and forced his own candidate, Pope Leo VIII, upon the Italians.

THE HOLY ROMAN EMPIRE (c. 970)

From this point on papal-imperial relations sank to degrading depths. Pope Boniface VII (984-985) had his predecessor, Benedict VI, strangled, stole the papal bank account and fled to Constantinople, hoping to buy the services of the Byzantines in his struggle against Emperor Otto II. When Otto II died, Boniface returned and imprisoned the newly elected Pope John XIV, who died of poisoning while in prison.

Otto III became emperor in 983 and appointed a close relative, Bruno, as Pope Gregory V. When the Italians overthrew Gregory for Pope John XVI, the 18-year-old emperor traveled to Rome, tortured and mutilated John, and paraded him through the streets of Rome. Through tactics such as this the German Ottos made it clear that they wanted nothing less than absolute control of the Church.

Otto III even moved to Rome and assumed permanent control of Church government. He freely appointed bishops to important sees. He also continued the policy of his father and grandfather by granting bishops and abbots independent control over their ecclesiastical properties, thereby binding the loyalty of these churchmen to the emperor rather than to the pope. Bishops, abbots and priests in the empire once again lived openly with large families, and Church property devolved upon the hereditary descendants of these prelates rather than upon men appointed from Rome.

The popes searched in vain for allies to help them restore papal control over Church affairs. The Italian nobility was of no help since it sought to make the papacy its own creation just as the Ottos had. In fact, when Otto III died in 1002, the various noble Italian families regained control of Italy and regularly vied with each other to place their own relatives on the papal throne, thus turning the papal office into a sinecure for their own interests.

Further Decline of Papal Prestige

When Otto III died his cousin Henry II succeeded him as emperor (1002-1024). Henry completely controlled episcopal appointments and regarded Church property as his own, selling it when his needs demanded. Henry remained in Germany, however, and as a result the powerful Tusculum family in Italy was able to gain control of the papacy.

One family member, Theophylact, was crowned as Pope Benedict VIII (1012-1024). Benedict was a skilled politician; he reached a working accord with the emperor in which Henry allowed the pope virtual independence in Italy. Benedict then turned his attention to dominating the other noble families in Italy, to waging war with the Spanish Moslems and to reforming the abuses in the institutional Church.

Emperor Henry and Pope Benedict met at Pavia in 1022 to

convene a reform synod. The chief topic on the agenda was the restoration of clerical celibacy. (For the origins of celibacy, see *The People of the Creed*, p. 141.)

Neither Henry nor Benedict was concerned with celibacy as a means to clerical sanctity. Their motives were more pragmatic. They both realized that hereditary descent of Church property created an administrative quagmire which served the interests of neither papacy nor empire. The Synod of Pavia thus decreed strict celibacy for all orders within the Church, from the subdiaconate on up. Slowly the celibacy decrees of Pavia began to take effect, especially when a universal reform effort began (as we shall see) shortly after Benedict's death.

A New Dynasty

When Emperor Henry II died childless in 1024 he was succeeded by Conrad II, the first member of a new imperial dynasty (the Salian Dynasty, 1024-1138). Pope Benedict VIII had died three months before Henry and was succeeded by his brother, a layman, who became Pope John XIX (1024-1033). (It was not at all unusual for a layman to be elected pope, ordained a priest and crowned as pope on the same day.) Emperor Conrad strengthened the imperial Church in Germany, as did his son and successor, Henry III (1039-1056). Henry III took many "proprietary" churches and abbeys (to be discussed shortly) away from their owners and ran them himself.

In Italy, the degradation of the papacy continued when—contrary to canon law—a 12-year-old became Pope Benedict IX (1033-1045). The Italian nobility continued to jostle each other for control of the papal office, and at one point Benedict IX was forced from the papal throne, replaced by Sylvester III, the candidate of a rival noble family. Benedict agreed to abdicate on condition that Sylvester's family reimburse him for the money he had spent to purchase the papal office in the first place.

A third family advanced another candidate as pope, who took the name Gregory VI. Emperor Henry III intervened in the conflict, deposing all three claimants and installing one of his own German bishops as Pope Clement II (1046-1047). From this moment on, Henry reestablished the policy of his ancestors by controlling all papal elections. The Italian nobility lost control of the papacy, and for several decades only German bishops were appointed as popes.

CHURCH-STATE RELATIONS:
TWO LEGAL SYSTEMS IN CONFLICT

The debasement of papal authority which we have just described was caused by more than human frailty and greed. Our image of the Church needs to be rounded out by other details, so that we gain a deeper historical understanding of the people and period. The key to understanding Church history from the mid-10th to the mid-12th centuries is the conflict between the Roman and Germanic concepts of law.

The Proprietary Church

During the early Carolingian period Frankish rulers developed a concept of the Church based on their own understanding of law which associated office and rights with ownership of property. From this developed an institution known as the "proprietary church." All churches, abbeys and chapels were owned and controlled by the owners ("proprietors") of the land on which they were built.

Proprietary churches were looked upon as a property right first and a religious institution second. The owner of the land controlled the churches and collected the surplus revenue they generated. The proprietor also paid for the upkeep of the bishops, abbots or priests who "staffed" *his* church. These proprietors were at the same time powerful lords in the service of the emperor, and thus the whole proprietary-church system was integrated into the imperial administration.

The proprietary church became the norm of ecclesiastical administration during the Carolingian, Saxon and Salien periods. This system was a natural outgrowth of Germanic law which saw the source of authority in the ownership of property. This clashed, however, with Roman canon law which provided that the bishop was to be appointed either by the pope or by a chief bishop of a province with the approval of the pope. According to canon law, the *office* of bishop and priest was the focal point of church authority—not the *ownership of Church property*.

Roman law viewed the property as existing for the support of the office. German law looked upon the situation from just the opposite perspective: The priest served the property rather than the property serving the priest.

The situation differed somewhat in towns and cities. There cathedral "chapters" (organizations of bishops and priests) controlled both the office and the property of urban cathedrals. Thus archbishops of great cities, such as Hincmar of Reims, could assert a good deal of independence from secular rulers in controlling both their churches and their episcopal offices.

Even in some rural areas, however, a few bishops gained a certain degree of independence where proprietors had no interest in overseeing their own churches. The main interest of such proprietors was simply to collect the revenue generated from episcopal taxation of priests and parishes. In some places, therefore, the proprietors gave the bishops a free hand in carrying out their duties of administering the sacraments and supervising priests and parishes. Nearly all proprietors, nevertheless, insisted on their chief prerogative, the appointment and investiture of new bishops.

Lay Investiture

Investiture was a technical term which denoted the act by which the proprietor gave to a new bishop his episcopal insignia—such as a crosier, miter and ring. Since property-law concepts predominated in this system, bishops and abbots had to pay for investiture, even though canon law specifically forbade such payments as simony. Bishops and abbots invested with their offices by proprietors became the latter's vassals and, like all other vassals in feudal Europe, were required to attend court at the proprietor's demand and to provide their lord-proprietor with soldiers when he needed them.

Outside of this investiture system stood one bishop, the bishop of Rome. Although popes were frequently appointed by the emperor during this period, they were not regarded by the emperors as feudal vassals, as were the bishops of the proprietary churches. Since the emperors looked upon the pope's authority as devolving from Peter directly, they did not conceive of the pope as bound by the investiture system. The emperors further realized that whatever was "Roman" about their own imperial offices stemmed from the lineage of the popes, whom the emperors regarded as both heirs and progenitors of the ancient Roman imperial dignity.

The popes, for their part, often succumbed to imperial control. Yet they still cherished the idea established by popes of the fourth and fifth centuries that a pope's right to control spiritual matters was superior to the rights of an emperor. The most subjugated medieval pope never relinquished this claim to spiritual supremacy over an emperor, even if he had to suppress the open espousal of such a claim.

The popes also held a special place in the minds of the Germanic peoples. As early as Merovingian times (the Frankish dynasty preceding the Carolingian; see p. 15), the Frankish tribes had greatly respected the popes and had developed a veritable cult of St. Peter which was centered in the person of the pope.

As the papacy saw it, the crisis for the Church was not just the emperors' attempt to dominate the papacy, but the emperors' control of the proprietary churches through the investiture system. Because of this system, non-Italian bishops and abbots were becoming increasingly independent from papal authority. A reform movement within monasticism, however, led to a reversal of this process.

The Cluniac Reform

Our brief discussion of papal-imperial conflict may give the impression that the entire Church between the mid-10th and mid-11th centuries suffered a steady moral decline. Such was not the case. Many voices protested the conflict between the ideal of the gospel and the actuality of Church life.

The chief sources of protest—and eventually of reform—were the monasteries. Yet before the monasteries could reform the Church at large, they had some housecleaning of their own to do.

Since the mid-ninth century, monasteries themselves had begun to experience moral decay. The chief reasons for this were the growing control of monasteries by lay proprietors, the frequent appointment by the proprietors of lay abbots who cared nothing for monastic discipline, and the attacks on monasteries by Norsemen, Moslems and Magyars (tribes from present-day Hungary).

Cluny

Out of this chaotic situation one monastery—Cluny—emerged as the leader of monastic reform. The reform at Cluny, in turn, led to general reform of the Church from the papacy on down.

Cluny was located in the Duchy of Burgundy, situated to the northwest of Italy between the Germanic territories controlled by the emperors and the old West-Frankish territories coming to be known as France (see map, p. 54). Cluny had itself been a proprietary abbey, founded in 910 by Duke William the Good of Aquitaine.

William had done a remarkable thing when he established Cluny. He guaranteed in the monastery's charter that Cluny would be free from all secular episcopal control, and that it would be under the direct authority of the papacy. Further, William guaranteed the free election of Cluny's abbots. When a man named Odo became abbot of Cluny (927-942), the monastery rapidly became a center for monastic reform. Eventually Cluny became one of the largest monasteries in all of Europe.

As Cluny's good reputation spread, the proprietors of other monasteries asked for assistance from Cluny to reform their own abbeys. Odo then brought 17 monasteries under Cluny's control; his successor abbots during the next century brought under Cluny's authority the majority of all the monasteries in Europe.

The Cluniac reform was based on a return to the strict observance of the Rule of St. Benedict as interpreted by Benedict of Aniane (see p. 47-48). The Cluniac monks observed strict silence and spent many hours praying and chanting in choir—in some places communally singing the entire psalter every day.

An integral part of the Cluniac reform was the right of each abbot to name his successor. Because of this the lay proprietors gradually lost control of abbatial investiture in Cluniac monasteries. The most significant element of the Cluniac movement, however, was that it brought vast numbers of previously independent proprietary abbeys under the direct control of the papacy.

The popes conferred special privileges on Cluny and its confederated houses. Pope Gregory V (996-999) in effect raised the dignity of Cluniac abbots above that of bishops by allowing the abbot of Cluny to choose which bishops would be permitted to visit at Cluny and celebrate Mass there. Pope John XIX (1024-1033) went even further by freeing Cluny's monks from the bishops' power to excommunicate. The Cluniac reform thus provided a means for the popes to reassert control of non-Italian bishops and to establish centers of papal authority north of the Alps.

The Cluniac reform stimulated reform-minded laypersons to demand overall Church reform. Some of the laity, so scandalized by the greed and immorality of the clergy, formed themselves into communities which came to resemble the Gnostic groups of the early Christian centuries (see *The People of the Creed*, p. 37). Such groups rejected marriage as evil, forbade the eating of meat, and formally repudiated the Church's sacramental system. On occasion they sacked churches and threw out relics and sacred art.

Calls for an End to Simony

Less extreme critics among the laity also vigorously protested the abuses in clerical celibacy and the continuing practice of simony. We get an understanding of how bad the practice of simony had become from the example set by the Count of Cerdagne. The count purchased the archbishopric of Narbonne for his 10-year-old son for 100,000 gold shillings (well over $1,000,000). The count had to outbid an abbot who—unknown to his brother monks—had embezzled the resources of his monastery in order to purchase the archepiscopal see for himself.

Such practices motivated not only the laity but many religious as well to demand the destruction of simony. A leading anti-simonian reformer, William of Volpiano, refused to take an oath of loyalty to his local bishop before being ordained as a deacon, on the grounds that such an oath was a form of simony. Such was the attitude of growing numbers of people concerning abuses within the Church.

At the heart of the protest over simony lay the conflict between the Germanic and Roman concepts of law discussed earlier. For the anti-simonists to succeed they would have to overcome the ancient Germanic concept of the king as theocratic ruler. Until control of the spiritual realm could be freed from secular domination, the Church would continue to degenerate and decay.

THE GREGORIAN REFORM

The struggle to reform the Church thus came to be symbolized in the papacy's struggle to win its freedom from imperial control. This struggle, which reaches its culmination in the reforms of Pope Gregory VII, began ironically during the very time when German popes held the papacy.

A feeble reform initiative was made when the German Pope Clement II (1046-1047) and Emperor Henry III—who had appointed Clement—convened a synod which condemned simony. No real penalties were imposed, however, for its practice. When Clement died, Henry appointed his friend, Bishop Bruno of Toul, as Pope Leo IX (1049-1054). Leo turned out to be an independent-minded man who regarded the papal office as a priestly calling rather than as an imperial footstool. With Leo, reform began in earnest.

Leo IX—the Prelude

Leo took a popular step with the Roman noble families, giving them the right to ratify his own appointment as pope, a right which they heartily accepted. (Until the fourth century the Roman bishops had been elected by Rome's citizens.) He then surrounded himself with talented bishops from every part of the empire. This court of advisers—which eventually evolved into a permanent "College of Cardinals"—traveled with Leo around Europe. In spending his papacy outside of Rome, Leo hoped to regain prestige for the papal office by making himself visible to more Christians, whose respect for the popes had been badly shaken during the past decades.

Leo's attack on Church corruption began by restoring celibacy.

He forbade his own flock in Rome from receiving priestly ministry from noncelibate priests and he ordered the mistresses of such priests into slavery. To combat simony Leo required all bishops and priests who had bought their offices to be reordained after appropriate penance and restitution.

When Pope Leo IX died, Emperor Henry III appointed another German as pope, Victor II. Victor continued Leo's reform by summoning reform synods at key cities throughout the empire and France. Instead of traveling around Europe like Leo had, however, Victor sent his own legates to oversee these reform synods. One such legate was a man named Hildebrand from Tuscany in northwestern Italy. Hildebrand would become Pope Gregory VII (1073-1085), the greatest champion of Church reform.

Gregory VII—the Culmination

Gregory was elected by the Roman nobility rather than appointed by the emperor. This was made possible because Henry III had died in 1056, leaving his six-year-old son, Henry IV, as successor; young Henry IV fell under the control of Duke Godfrey of Lorraine, a supporter of Hildebrand. When Hildebrand became pope, the papacy momentarily came out from under the emperor's thumb.

Gregory, who had been a Cluniac monk, continued to wear his monk's habit as pope and freely used Cluniac monks to advance his reform. Seeing the Church's freedom from secular control as the key to reform, he reasserted the ancient papal claim of superiority over the emperor in spiritual matters. Like his namesake, Gregory the Great (d. 604), Gregory VII developed a theory of papal sovereignty based on the popes' lineal descent from Peter. Gregory believed that in a very real sense Peter lived on in each pope. The apostle, Gregory said, transferred to each of his successors his own merits, enabling the popes to rule in true apostolic fashion.

In a series of "Dictates," Gregory reasserted the primacy of Rome and the right of the Roman Church to decide ecclesiastical controversies. Gregory further decreed that the pope, as heir of Peter's sanctity, was endowed by Christ to "bind and loose" not only in spiritual matters but in temporal affairs as well. In a monumental assertion of power, he assumed for himself the right to depose secular rulers and to exonerate a ruler's subjects from their feudal oaths of fealty. It remained to be seen whether Gregory's theories could be imposed in practice.

Gregory convened his first reform synod in 1074, expelling from office all clergy who had purchased their ordinations and making clerical celibacy an absolute requirement. In 1078 he took the fateful step of ruling that no bishop or abbot could be invested with office by a layman. Thus began the great *investiture controversy* which rocked Church and empire for several decades.

The Investiture Controversy

Gregory's decision on lay investiture had been precipitated by the action of Emperor Henry IV (now 23 and in command of the imperial government). In 1073 he had invested the archbishop of Milan with the episcopal insignia. Henry was supported in this by his own German bishops, who in 1076 sent Gregory a letter defying his authority over them. Henry ordered Gregory to resign, but Gregory responded by excommunicating the emperor and relieving his German subjects from their oaths of fealty.

Powerful German princes seized upon this opportunity to challenge Emperor Henry's power, and so came out in support of Pope Gregory. They invited the pope to Germany to attend a Diet (legislative assembly) to settle the controversy. Henry wanted at all costs to avoid an alliance between the pope and his own ambitious German barons, so he set out to block Gregory's passage across the Alps and to beg the pope's forgiveness. At Canossa in northern Italy, Henry appeared before Gregory's castle dressed as a penitent. According to the popular account, Henry stood barefoot in the snow for three days until Gregory received him back into the Church.

Henry changed his mind as soon as he left Canossa. In 1081 he marched on Rome, winning to his side 13 cardinals and the Roman populace, who had wearied of the puritan Gregory. Henry installed his own pope, Clement III, and Gregory fled to Norman-occupied southern Italy, where he died in 1085 lamenting, "I have loved justice and hated iniquity; therefore I die in exile."

Victory at Worms

Although Gregory lost the battle, through his successors he won the war. The scene of the emperor's humiliation at Canossa was imprinted into the consciousness of every ambitious prince in the empire, and it inspired future popes to carry on Gregory's reform program. When Emperor Henry IV again became embroiled with rebellious princes at home, Pope Urban II (1088-1099) reasserted the Gregorian reform. In 1095 he reinstituted Gregory's prohibition against lay investiture of bishops and abbots.

Urban's successor, Paschal II, made an alliance with King Louis VI of France in which the king agreed to renounce lay investiture in his realm. The new German emperor, Henry V, besieged by troubles on every side, found the pope's growing strength too much to take. In 1122 Henry V negotiated with Pope Calixtus II an end to the investiture controversy. By the *Concordat of Worms* (pronounced "Vorms"—the German town where the settlement was effected), Henry renounced his right to invest bishops with ring and staff and guaranteed canonical episcopal elections and consecration free of simony.

The *Concordat of Worms* shattered the imperial-controlled Church established by Otto I and his successors. German bishops and abbots now came under the papacy's direct control. The belief in theocratic kingship suffered a severe blow, and the papacy emerged as a powerful monarchy in its own right. A new era had begun. The possibility of a truly integrated and universal Christendom—of a spiritual Kingdom on earth under the leadership of Peter's successor—began to take hold of the medieval mind.

CHAPTER FIVE

BYZANTIUM'S BREAK WITH THE WEST

Toward Schism (962-1054)

In this chapter we will focus on developments within the Byzantine Church during the same time period covered by our discussion of the Western Church in the last chapter. The most significant event within the Eastern Church during this time was its schism with Rome.

THE HISTORICAL BACKDROP

The tensions between Rome and Constantinople were greatly exacerbated by the fact that Western kings had assumed the title and prerogatives of the Roman emperor (see p. 3). From the Byzantine point of view, Charlemagne's coronation as emperor in 800 had been bad enough; but the coronation of Otto I in 962 proved even worse.

Otto was determined to eliminate once and for all the Byzantine claim to Italian lands. This would eradicate any basis Byzantium still had for regarding itself as the true successor to the universal Roman Empire. (Recall that Otto had given the papacy a large parcel of land in Italy, much of it still claimed by the Byzantines.) To add to the Easterners' woes, a new force had emerged to challenge the former Byzantine control of Sicily and southern Italy: the Normans.

The Norman Threat

Barbarian pirates from Scandinavia known as Norsemen had been successful in consolidating their control over a large region in the northwest of France. About the year 911 these Scandinavians gained formal recognition from the Frankish King Charles the Simple for the possession of a large duchy which would come to bear their name—Normandy. The Normans accepted Christianity, but continued their restless, conquering travels. It was Duke William of Normandy who defeated the Anglo-Saxons at Hastings in 1066 to become King William I of England. During the 11th century the Normans also seized all of southern Italy and challenged both Moslems and Byzantines for control of Sicily.

The Normans befriended the reforming popes; they had offered Pope Gregory VII a safe haven in Salerno when Emperor Henry IV drove him from Rome (see p. 63). But to the Byzantines the Normans, Christian or not, represented (along with the Moslems) just one more threat to Byzantine power in the West. Relations between Rome and Constantinople worsened when Pope Benedict VIII supported Norman conquest of Byzantine lands in southern Italy; tensions reached the boiling point under the Byzantine patriarch (Archbishop of Constantinople) Michael Cerularius (1043-1058).

Patriarch vs. Pope

Archbishop Michael staunchly defended the independence of his patriarchate from the supervision of Rome and condemned the concept of papal primacy in angry, harsh words. He pointed to the virtual seizure of the papacy by the German emperors as demonstrable proof that God had not divinely endowed Rome with any special prerogatives above the other bishops of Christendom. Because of the growing theological controversies between East and West (discussed below), Michael advanced the contrary claim—that it was Constantinople and not Rome which infallibly preserved the ancient faith.

Michael stepped up his anti-Latin campaign by closing all Western (Latin-rite) churches in Constantinople. He also demanded that the pope stop all liturgical practices deemed heretical by the East. In an attempt to heal the rift between the two Churches, Pope Leo IX sent a delegation to Constantinople in 1054 headed by Cardinal-Bishop Humbert.

Leo's motives were political as well as religious. Relations between the papacy and the Normans had soured since the time of Pope Benedict VIII; at one point the Normans had even taken Pope Leo captive. Thus, Pope Leo hoped that Humbert could drum up Byzantine support for the papacy's conflict with the Normans.

Humbert was not the right man to send to Constantinople on a mission of reconciliation. He arrived in the city and began issuing orders to Byzantine bishops as if they were his servants. He proudly displayed a list of more than 90 heresies of which the Byzantine Church was said to be guilty.

Patriarch Michael fought venom with venom, and the Roman delegation decided to leave without even negotiating with the Byzantines. Before they left, on July 16, 1054, the Romans laid on the altar of the Great Basilica of Hagia Sophia ("Holy Wisdom") a decree solemnly excommunicating Michael and declaring various Byzantine beliefs and practices to be heretical. The decree called Michael and his supporters Simonists, Arians and Manicheans.* It also condemned the Byzantine teaching on the procession of the Holy Spirit (discussed below), as well as the practice of allowing Byzantine priests to be married.

It is interesting to note that since Pope Leo IX had died three months before Humbert's actions, the decree of excommunication must be read as Humbert's own doing and not the pope's. Also, the decree attacked only Patriarch Michael and certain Eastern practices, *not* the Byzantine Church as such. Yet, in Michael's hands, that is how the Romans' statement was interpreted.

Michael responded with an excommunication of Humbert and his legates, but not of the pope or the Roman Church. Formally and legally, therefore, nothing had been done to bring the two Churches into a state of schism. Yet, because of the harshness of the denunciations issued by both sides, Christians in East and West assumed that a formal break had taken place. As this mentality took hold, it gradually became accurate to speak of a "schism" having occurred and to date the schism from the year 1054. As we shall see, Rome and Constantinople unsuccessfully continued to attempt reconciliation on several other occasions before the final collapse of the Byzantine state in 1453 (see p. 145).

THE THEOLOGICAL ISSUES

The Question of Papal Authority
Having summarized the external features of the schism, we now turn to its underlying theological causes. Probing these provides a good overview of Byzantine theology from the ninth to the 11th century.

The Eastern attitude toward Roman primacy had not always been one of hostility. The Eastern bishops had respected the Roman bishops'

---

* Arians taught that Christ was not of equal divinity with the Father. Manicheans believed the world was ruled by two supreme spirits, one good and one evil.

67

claim to speak with Peter's authority, as clearly exemplified by their acclamation at the Council of Chalcedon (451) that in Pope Leo's *Tome* "Peter has spoken" (see *The People of the Creed*, p. 102).

In fact, the Easterners could not conceive of a major Church decision being reached without the participation of the Roman bishop. Their disagreement with Rome was over the papacy's claim to be the *sole* voice for Christian orthodoxy. We might summarize the Easterners' attitude toward relations with the papacy as "Collaboration, yes! Domination, no!"

One aspect of Rome's claim to primacy was Rome's spotless record on the doctrinal controversies which had rocked the Church during its first six centuries. Rome had always supported the eventual orthodox position on the various theological controversies. Indeed, in contrast to the East, the Western Church looked like a calm bastion of steadfast certainty during the very times when the Eastern Church had splintered into angry factions. To Western theologians this propensity for the Roman see constantly to advance the correct viewpoint was abundant evidence that the Roman Church was the final, infallible voice of Christian authority.

This argument for Roman primacy had great effect, even in the East, until the tenure of Pope Honorius I (625-638). During his papacy the Byzantine Emperor Heraclius engaged in one more fruitless effort to reconcile the Monophysites—those in the East who believed that Christ had only one nature—with the Chalcedonians—those who advanced the majority view of Christ as "one person in two natures."

Emperor Heraclius almost worked out a compromise between Monophysites and Chalcedonians when he proposed a formula which asserted two natures in Christ but only one mode of activity, or "one energy." Heraclius referred the formula for approval to his patriarch, Sergius, who in turn sought out the opinion of Pope Honorius. The "one energy" formula admitted that there were two natures in Christ, but it attributed only one mode of behavior—that of the divine Word—to the humanity of Jesus.

In other words, by this formula Jesus the man was said to have expended no human energy in carrying out his activities. Rather, everything Jesus did came from the Word's divine energy at work in him. Pope Honorius wrote back a hasty reply to Sergius in which he proposed a formula of "one will" in Christ rather than "one energy," and ordered all parties to cease their dispute.

Bolstered by Honorius's formula, Emperor Heraclius in 638 issued the *Ecthesis* ("statement of faith") in which he forbade any further talk about "energies" and adopted Honorius's formula of "one will."

The *Ecthesis* was then approved by two councils held in Constantinople, in 638 and 639.

Thus, Monotheletism (from the Greek for "one will") became the Church's official teaching—but only for a short while. Pope Honorius's successors, Pope Severinus and Pope John IV, repudiated Honorius's teaching, and the Council of Constantinople in 681 condemned both Pope Honorius and Monotheletism. The council—supported by Rome—substituted a new formula proclaiming the existence in Christ of two wills, human and divine.

The significance of all this was to call into question for the first time the judgment of a pope in deciding a doctrinal controversy. In effect, it marked the beginning of the end of the Easterners' respect for papal teaching, and led to grave suspicion within the Eastern Church concerning all future papal pronouncements. To their credit, Western theologians candidly admitted that Pope Honorius had erred, and they rejected his doctrine as vociferously as did the Easterners. Pope Leo II (681-683), for example, accused Honorius of "having tried to subvert the immaculate faith by his utter treachery."[1]

Gradually, a strenuous theological debate began to develop over the concept of papal authority. The battleground was the familiar Scripture verse, Matthew 16:18: "...you are 'Rock,' and on this rock I will build my church...." Byzantine theologians developed an exegesis of this verse which identified the "rock" (upon which Jesus wanted to build his Church) with Peter's confession of faith rather than with Peter himself. Thus, the rock upon which the Church is built, according to the Byzantines, was not Peter and his successors but Peter's *faith*, which all Christians possess. To the Byzantines the bishop of Rome was to be respected as any other bishop so long as his faith remained orthodox.

In contradistinction to papal primacy, the Byzantines developed the doctrine of the *pentarchy*. This proposed that not one but *five* ancient sees possessed jurisdiction over questions of doctrine and, by extension, over ecclesiastical administration and government. These five sees were Rome, Constantinople, Jerusalem, Antioch and Alexandria. One weakness of this doctrine lay in the fact that the Church in Constantinople had no real claim to apostolic foundation, even though a legend attributed the founding of the Church in Byzantium (the first-century name for Constantinople) to the Apostle Andrew. Byzantines used this legend along with John 1:40-42 (Andrew's introduction of Peter to Christ) to argue that, since Andrew had brought Peter to Christ, it was Constantinople and not Rome which possessed ecclesiastical primacy.

Differences in Doctrine and Liturgy

Along with the seemingly insoluble problem of Church authority, there were several doctrinal and liturgical differences dividing East and West, most of which we might regard as trival. But the Easterners and Westerners, already suspicious of each other, magnified even minute points of disagreement into major quarrels. Let's briefly summarize the chief differences.

1) Administration of Confirmation. In the East the local parish priest administered the Sacrament of Confirmation, while in the West the bishop administered it. This petty distinction had resulted simply from the fact that in the early Church Eastern bishops had supervised larger territories than their Western confreres and thus needed to delegate more authority to their priests. Further, the Eastern Church had developed the custom of administering Confirmation immediately after Baptism. In this practice the bishop merely consecrated the oil and handed it to the priest who performed the actual anointing. In the West, on the other hand, the bishop was the regular minister of both Baptism and Confirmation. He eventually relinquished the former but not the latter ministry to his priests.

2) Celibacy. The West, as we have seen, required strict celibacy of its priests (even if celibacy was often not practiced), while the East allowed clerical marriage. The question asked by one Byzantine theologian typified the East's bewilderment over the West's requirement of priestly celibacy: "What kind of teacher of the Church was it who handed on such an absurd tradition to you?"[2] In actuality, there had been an early tradition even in the East requiring clerical celibacy which by the 10th century had simply died out.

3) Frequency of Eucharist. Priests in the West increasingly tended to celebrate Mass daily, while in the East priests generally celebrated Mass only on Sunday or feast days. The distinction arose from the differing emphases placed on the Mass in East and West. Westerners more and more looked on the Mass as a sacrifice—thus the more it was celebrated the better. Easterners, however, focused on the communal-worship aspect and, since the entire community could not gather except on Sundays and holy days, they usually reserved Mass for those occasions.

4) Emphasis on Icons. Although Westerners were certainly not iconoclasts, icons did not play the central role in Western liturgies that they played in the East. One Byzantine theologian complained that "the Latins do not set up representatives of the saints, except for the crucifixion, in their churches."[3] (This was, in fact, inaccurate; Western churches were often adorned with statues of the saints.)

5) Leavened vs. Unleavened Bread. A major cause of discord between East and West concerned the West's use of unleavened bread ("azymes") in the Eucharist as contrasted with the East's use of leavened bread. Although such a distinction may strike us as insignificant, to one prominent Byzantine theologian this liturgical difference was "...the principal cause of the division between them and us....the matter of azymes involves in summary form the whole question of true piety; if it is not cured, the disease of the Church cannot be cured."[4]

This controversy stemmed from the fact that East and West had different attitudes toward the use of the Old Testament in the celebration of the Mass. The West focused on types (prefigurements) of the Eucharist in the Old Testament and their fulfillment in the New Testament. The manna which fed the Israelites in the desert, for example, was said to be a "type" of the Eucharist. Because of this focus on Old Testament types, the Latins professed to keep the Jewish custom of eating unleavened bread in the Eucharist, just as the Jews had eaten unleavened bread at Passover.

According to the Byzantines, however, the Latins celebrated Mass "Mosaically," still "eating at the table of the Jews."[5] Western theologians responded to this charge by saying that they were merely following Christ's own example, who during the days of Passover could not have found "leavened bread in all the territory of Israel."[6]

6) Two Different Languages. With the increasing Moslem invasions of Byzantine territory, communications with the West were often cut off. As a result, linguistic developments were not adequately communicated between the two Churches. The Byzantines constantly criticized the West's ignorance of Greek. Yet the very "heirs of the Roman Empire" in Constantinople knew little, if any, Latin.

Because of their ignorance of each other's languages, East and West relied exclusively on their own respective written traditions when engaging the other side in theological debate. Thus little interpenetration of the Greek and Latin patristic writings took place between East and West. Patriarch Michael Cerularius, for example, complained that the Westerners "do not count our saintly and great Fathers, theologians, and high priests among the other saints"[7] (an erroneous charge—consider Erigena, p. 41), while Westerners were regularly amazed to find that Byzantine theologians knew little of Augustine.

THE *FILIOQUE* DISPUTE

The most intractable theological controversy between East and West involved a single Latin word, *filioque*, which means "and the

71

son." The Creed of Constantinople (381) had stated that the Holy Spirit "proceeds from the Father." The Western addition of "and the Son" to this formula can be traced to the Third Council of Toledo (589). The Synod of Frejus (796) also defended its usage. From about 800 on in the West, when the creed came to be recited regularly at Mass, the *filioque*'s place in the Latin liturgy was assured.

To the Byzantines, for whom reliance on the literal wording of the great creeds was an essential element of Christian orthodoxy, the Western addition of *filioque* was both an insult and a heresy. Patriarch Michael Cerularius called the West's use of *filioque* "wicked and dangerous."[8] The Byzantine theologian Peter of Antioch called the *filioque* "a wicked thing, and among the wicked things the most wicked."[9]

'Sending' or 'Proceeding'?

To the East, the West's insertion of *filioque* into the creed was an act of "extreme effrontery" and an "adulteration" of the holy and sacred creed. Byzantines considered the central error of the *filioque* to be its confusion of the difference between the "sending" and the "proceeding" of the Holy Spirit. While it was accurate to say the Son *sent* the Holy Spirit (quoting such passages as John 16:7), the Byzantines said it was a grave error to say the Son in effect *begot* the Holy Spirit, which is how they interpreted the West's use of the *filioque*.

The Byzantines were correct in stating that Western theologians equated the proceeding and the sending of the Holy Spirit. Pope Gregory the Great, for example, had written that the Spirit's "being sent is the very procession by which he proceeds from the Father and the Son."[10] And Ratramnus of Corbie had equated the *sending* in John 15:26 with the word *comes* in the same passage—"the Spirit of truth who *comes* from the Father" (emphasis added).

Augustine on the Trinity

The distinction between East and West over the *filioque* essentially came down to two different ways of looking at the Trinity. Augustine had written that the Holy Spirit "referred both to the Father and to the Son, because the Holy Spirit is the Spirit both of the Father and of the Son."[11] Augustine, remember, had stressed the unity of the entire Trinity in the actions of any of the three persons (see *The People of the Creed*, p. 126). Thus, for him and for future Western theologians, to isolate the Spirit from the Son by denying the Spirit's procession from both Father and Son would amount to denying the unity of the Trinity.

The Byzantines agreed with the West that the unity of the Trinity must be preserved, but they saw this unity coming only from the Father, who was the only person in the Trinity without a "source." To say that the Spirit proceeds from both Father and Son, the Byzantines said, is to posit two sources within the "Godhead."

Two Different Views of God

The introduction of the word *Godhead* into the debate made each side's arguments more divergent. For the Westerners, the only Godhead was the Trinity itself—the one, unified essence of God in three persons. By saying that only the Father was the "source" or the "cause" of the Son and the Spirit, Byzantine theologians seemed at times to suggest that the Godhead and the Father were identical.

Would this mean, then, that there exists a Godhead which is somehow beyond and transcendent to the Trinity? Byzantine mystical writings seemed at times to suggest such an idea, as when Pseudo-Dionysius and his successors spoke of God as the ultimate mystery, beyond any dogmatic definitions. Western theologians were too dependent on Augustine to conceive of a Godhead not completely identified with the Trinity.

We could generalize the distinctions between the views of God in East and West by saying that the East constantly asserted God's mystery and transcendence—his "other-ness"—while the West emphasized God as person—as manifested in God's own interpersonal relationship within the Trinity. The West, therefore, tended to focus on God's immanence, his "here-and-now-ness," and saw God as community in unity. The East's penchant for mysticism, however, led Byzantine theologians to stress God's absolute one-ness beyond all relationship.

THE BYZANTINE LEGACY

The conflict over papal authority, the differing doctrinal and liturgical practices and, above all, the controversy over the *filioque* drove Rome and Constantinople ever farther apart, so that from the Schism of 1054 onward it became impossible to effectuate a true reunion.

It would take more than a century for Western theologians to have regular access to the sources of Eastern mystical theology and, thus, for the West to develop a spirituality more harmonious with that of the East (as we see on p. 158). If this development had taken place sooner—if Humbert and his colleagues, for example, had been able to appreciate the riches of Byzantine spirituality—the Schism of 1054 would likely not have taken place.

What was this Byzantine spiritual legacy that the Westerners had misunderstood and failed to appreciate? Because of their mystical bent Byzantine Christians believed that faith was not so much an "it"—that is, a body of objective doctrine—as it was a relationship between the human spirit and God's own spirit. Through this relationship, Byzantine mystics felt that one became a whole and integrated person, a person who experienced the "love which surpasses all knowledge, so that [one could] attain to the fullness of God himself" (Ephesians 3:19).

Byzantine spirituality was thus based on the premise that holiness is dependent upon wholeness, upon an experiential union with God in which "all of us, gazing on the Lord's glory with unveiled faces, are being transformed from glory to glory into his very image by the Lord who is the Spirit" (2 Corinthians 3:18). This conviction of the Byzantine spiritual masters that holiness and wholeness could be attained only through contemplative experience would have a profound influence on Western spirituality.

At the very time when Scholastic theologians were writing their great treatises—when they were establishing "the faith" as the content of objective doctrine—other Western Christians were absorbing the Eastern mystical tradition and translating that tradition into Western terminology. In hindsight we can now appreciate Byzantine spirituality as the greatest legacy donated to Western Christianity by the East.

CHAPTER SIX

A NEW APPROACH TO OLD DOCTRINE

Early Scholasticism

As papacy and emperor struggled for dominance in Western Europe (see Chapter Four), an entirely new way of thinking was developing there. Known as Scholasticism, this system was not so much the elaboration of a new body of doctrine as a new method by which theologians approached the old doctrines. The purpose of the Scholastic method was to arrive at a deeper understanding of revealed truth through the use of reason.

THE ORIGINS OF SCHOLASTICISM

Augustine, in a sense, could be named the founder of Scholasticism since he was the first significant Western thinker to speak of the compatibility between faith and reason in the exposition of doctrine. "To believe is to ponder with assent," he wrote and, "Understand so that you may believe; believe so that you may understand."

After Augustine we should list Erigena as another pioneer in the development of Scholasticism. His use of dialectic (see p. 42) laid the groundwork for the method of argumentation which all Scholastics would use. Yet not until the 11th century did a genius arise who developed a more systematic method which could truly be identified as medieval Scholasticism. That genius was Anselm of Canterbury (1033-1109), the "Father of Scholasticism."

Anselm of Canterbury

Anselm had been educated by the Benedictines. He became abbot of the monastery of Bec in Normandy and then archbishop of Canterbury in England. Anselm was first and last an Augustinian, but he was attracted less to the first clause of Augustine's maxim—"understand so that you may believe"—than to the second clause—"believe so that you may understand." For Anselm, all theological speculation was based on assent to revealed truths which led, by way of dialectic, to a systematic and rational statement of those truths.

To get some idea of how Anselm applied dialectic to the formulation of theology, consider his famous "ontological proof" for the existence of God. (*Ontology* is the study of being.) We could outline Anselm's proof, using the dialectical procedure developed by Erigena, as follows:

Major Premise:	God is a being "than which no greater can be thought"; that is, our thought of God is a thought of a perfect being.
Minor Premise:	If God existed only in our thought of him, however, he would not truly be perfect, because a truly perfect being would possess existence as one of his attributes.
Conclusion:	Hence, our thought of God is a thought of a truly existing perfect being; that is, God exists.

Why Scholasticism?

One might wonder why anyone felt it necessary to use logic and reason in the formulation of doctrine. Keep in mind several points: First of all, scholars in the early Middle Ages possessed a strong desire to keep the early patristic tradition from dying out. Since that tradition itself had largely been formed from the conflict between pagan philosophy (reason) and Christian revelation (faith), the medieval copyists imbibed, as it were, the argumentative methods of the Fathers.

Second, during the Carolingian heyday a scholarly revival known as the "Carolingian Renaissance" gave birth to a new way of relating to the patristic writings. Scholars moved from mere copying or editing to interpretation, as we saw earlier (see p. 37).

Finally, as this new interpretative look at the Fathers resulted in theological controversies (see Chapter Three), it became necessary once again—as in the days of the early Church—to employ reason and logic in combating heresy and defining doctrine.

THEOLOGICAL CONCERNS

The early Scholastics—theologians who were influenced by Anselm and his method—turned their attention to the traditional issues raised by Christian revelation and, in particular, to two broad categories of that revelation: (1) how Christ saves humanity; and (2) how humanity avails itself of Christ's act of salvation.

How Does Christ Save Humanity?

This category of Scholastic inquiry is well summarized in the title of Anselm's famous treatise, *Why God Became Man*. As the title suggests, Anselm and his fellow Scholastics wanted to develop a rational understanding of the Christ-event. Let's look briefly at how they proceeded.

1) The Paradox: Justice vs. Mercy. For the Scholastics, the concept of salvation contained a paradox: God's justice clashes with his mercy. By justice the Scholastics meant God's innate holiness, which is absolutely unchangeable. God's justice requires that he be eternally steadfast for, if God could change, if he could say yes today and no tomorrow, then his absolute holiness would be subject to external influence. If one moment God condemns sinners (expelling Adam and Eve from Eden), and the next moment he forgives sinners (in Jesus' death on the cross), could not one logically conclude that God is not unchangeable? As the Scholastic Peter Abelard (1079-1142) reasoned, when change takes place, being and non-being come together and, if this were true of God, then he is not absolute after all.

2) The Solution: 'Satisfaction.' The Scholastics resolved the paradox in the following way. Originally, they said, the just, unchanging God had created a just, unchanging creature. Yet, with the Fall, humanity had chosen to separate from God. At this point, humanity became "divided," as Anselm put it; men and women had within them the capacity for God's own justice, but they had chosen to live in a state of non-justice, or sin.

With the Fall, God's justice remained unchanged; it was only humanity which had suffered a loss. To recoup this loss humanity had to repay God that which it had destroyed by sinning—namely, the justice which Adam had shared with God. Anselm called this repayment "satisfaction." And upon his theory of satisfaction Anselm constructed his theory of the means by which humanity returns to its lost state of unchanging wholeness.

By Adam's fall, rightness and order had been violated, leaving God with only two choices: eternal punishment for those who had violated God's order, or satisfaction for Adam's sin and a restoration of order. God's justice demanded the first alternative; God's mercy necessitated the second alternative. In the divine-human union of Jesus Christ the paradox of justice and mercy was resolved.

A Scholastic thinker who understood Anselm's thought, Rupert of Deutz, put it this way: "Because no one owed satisfaction for guilt except man and because no one could render it except a merciful God, God became man, who, because he did not owe anything in his own name, discharged our debt by dying for us."[1]

How Do We Receive Christ's Grace?

Once the Scholastics had resolved the paradox of justice and mercy, they were in a better position to answer the more practical question: How do we avail ourselves of Christ's satisfaction for sin? Or, how do we receive Christ's grace? Let's look briefly at the chief sources of Christ's grace discussed by the Scholastics.

1) Mary as Mediatrix. In the 11th and 12th centuries Mariology became a central concern of Scholastic inquiry. Theologians ascribed to Mary the highest merits and privileges. The list of her honorific titles proliferated: "Queen of Angels," "Mother of Truth," "Mother of Christians." Baldwin of Canterbury, in comparing her to other women, exclaimed that Mary was "more beautiful than all of them, more lovable than all of them, supersplendid, supergracious, superglorious!"[2]

Much of this had been said before. What distinguished early Scholastic Mariology was its elaboration upon the idea of Mary as mediatrix. The Scholastics based this idea on two propositions that they had deduced from their discussion of Christ as redeemer: (1) Had it not been for Mary there would have been no savior and, thus, no redemption by which people could have been saved. (2) Through Mary, Christ was given to us; therefore, it is through Mary that we in turn give ourselves to Christ. For Baldwin, Mary was "the minister and cooperator of this dispensation, who gave us the salvation of the world."[3]

Mary was said to be the means by which people came to know and accept Christ. Thus Peter Damian could ask of Mary, "By your pious prayer make your son propitious to us,"[4] and Bernard of Clairvaux echoed, "Our Lady, our mediatrix, our advocate, reconcile us to your son...through the prerogatives that you have merited, through the mercy to which you have given birth."[5]

Such language naturally raised the question of the relationship between Christ and Mary in the plan of salvation. Did Mary's title of "mediatrix" detract from Christ's role as the "one mediator" (1 Timothy 2:5) between God and humanity?

The Scholastics interpreted Mary's prerogative as mediatrix solely as a grace conferred by Christ. Anselm, for example, cautioned against "Mariolatry" by reminding his readers that Mary was "exalted" *through* Christ. All that was predicated of Mary came from Christ and his grace of redemption. She was not the source of merit in herself, but conferred merit only insofar as she had been graced in this capacity by Christ.

This inevitably returned the Scholastics to the question raised by earlier theologians concerning the degree to which Mary had been graced and the moment when her special privilege of grace had been given to her. Bernard of Clairvaux argued against Mary's immaculate conception. If Mary had been conceived differently from other human beings, he reasoned, then there would have been no need for Christ to bestow his special prerogatives on her—since she would have already possessed these prerogatives by nature.

Other theologians disagreed. How, they asked, could Jesus' birth have been sinless if his mother's had not been sinless?

While there continued to be differing opinions on Mary's sinless conception, there was general agreement, however, on the question of her assumption into heaven. This was due principally to the fact that there had long been a liturgical feast celebrating the Assumption but no comparable feast for the Immaculate Conception.

2) The Saints. The idea that Mary was mediatrix between humanity and Christ and a source of Christ's grace was extended by the Scholastics to lesser holy men and women who had gone to heaven. Of course this belief, like the devotion to Mary, was nothing new. The Scholastics merely systematized a very old idea—that of the communion of the saints.

The worshiping body on earth, Bernard said, were "fellow citizens and comrades of the blessed spirits."[6] And just as prayers could be addressed to Mary, so too it was a true act of devotion to pray to the saints. Scholastic theology thus drew together heaven and earth into one united community within God's Kingdom. The Scholastics saw communion with the saints as a means to human wholeness.

Because there was merit to be gained by prayer to the saints and imitation of their lives, Christians attached great importance to the tangible relics of the saints' bodies, clothing or personal effects. And, since so many miracles were associated with the cult of relics, medieval Christians generally assumed that the power of a relic was the power of the saint.

The question then arose as to whether merit derived from the intercession of the saint in heaven or simply from contact with the relic itself. Theologians were tentative and vague in their responses, as when Odo of Cluny, questioned about miraculous healings ascribed to a relic of St. Gerald, responded, "The benefits of health are conferred through the holy relics in such a way as not to deny the cooperating virtue of St. Gerald."[7]

Without a clear-cut theology of relics, the laity's imagination frequently ran wild, and a good deal of fakery became associated with the cult of saints and relics. Preachers held up before their awed congregations "a portion of the bread that the Lord chewed with his very own teeth,"[8] and one monastery was renowned because it possessed the baby Jesus' first teeth.

Theologians realized that an unbridled fascination with relics would lead to a conflict in Christian doctrine concerning the preeminence of the Eucharist as the supreme "relic" of Christ's presence. One story tells of a knight who, when chided by his bishop for taking a bite out of the forearm bone of a noted saint, responded, "I have just eaten all of Christ's body in the Mass. How can munching on the saint's relic constitute an impiety?"

3) The Real Presence. During this period discussion of the Eucharist focused on *how* the miracle of the Real Presence took place. The Scholastics began using the word *substance* rather than the ninth-century word *figure* (see p. 40). *Substance* meant virtually the same thing as "essence" or "being," and it now became popular to speak of the miracle of the Eucharistic conversion as a transformation of substance. Baldwin of Canterbury, for example, defined the new position by saying, "The substance of the bread is changed into the substance of the flesh of Christ."[9] Baldwin's position was but a further development of the Eucharistic theology of Radbertus of Corbie (see pp. 40-41).

The first person to coin the term *transubstantiation* ("transformation of substance") was Pope Alexander III. Prior to becoming pope (as professor Orlando Bandinelli of the University of Bologna), he used the word in a treatise in the year 1140. The Fourth Lateran Council defined Alexander's formula as official doctrine in 1215, declaring: "The body and blood of Jesus Christ are truly contained in the sacrament of the altar under the outward appearances of bread and wine, the bread having been *transubstantiated* into the body and the wine into the blood"[10] (emphasis added). The Council of Trent reasserted this dogmatic formula in 1551; it has remained Catholic dogma to this day.

4) The Seven Sacraments. The Scholastic discussion of the Eucharistic presence naturally affected the entire theory of the sacraments. The debate over the Eucharist tended to place the Eucharist at center stage, as it were, so that the previous centrality of Baptism in the sacramental system diminished. A monk of Cluny, Alger of Liege (d. 1132), evaluated the two sacraments as follows: "The water of Baptism does not contain the Holy Spirit essentially, but only figuratively; only the sacrament of bread and wine is changed in such a way that in substance it is not what it used to be before."[11]

The Eucharistic controversy inspired Scholastics to analyze and define the concept of sacrament as such. Following Augustine, Pope Alexander III wrote that "a sacrament is the visible sign of the invisible grace."[12]

It was a simple matter to apply this definition to sacraments such as Baptism, Eucharist and Anointing of the Sick, which had tangible *signs*, but more difficult to apply it to, for example, Penance or Matrimony, which had not previously been considered as sacraments and which had no signs as such. Scholastic theologians thus introduced a new element into sacramental theology: the *matter* of the sacrament. In Penance, for example, the matter of the sacrament was said to be the telling of sins, contrition and satisfaction.

Along with sign and matter, another key element of sacramental theology became the sacrament's *means of institution*. Hugh of St. Victor (d. 1142) formulated the principle that a sacrament had to be instituted by Christ. This created difficulty for some sacraments. Scripture contained four accounts of Christ's institution of the Eucharist (Matthew 26:26-28; Mark 14:22-24; Luke 22:19-20; 1 Corinthians 11:23-25) and at least three references by Christ to Baptism (Matthew 3:13-15; 28:19 ; John 3:5), but Christ's institution of other sacraments was less certain. John 20:23 was cited as authority for the Sacrament of Penance, although James 5:16 suggested that the actual confession of sins was not related to the priestly ministry. And in fact, it was a custom all during the Middle Ages for Christians to confess their sins to one another as well as to a priest.

The first listing of *seven* sacraments dates to an anonymous treatise published in 1145, *The Sentences of Divinity*, which listed the seven known today. Peter Lombard (1100-1160) finalized this number in his *Sentences*, a famous textbook which became the standard for theological instruction well into the 16th century. In Lombard's theology, each sacrament came to be seen as a channel of a unique grace.

By linking the seven sacraments with Mary's mediation and the communion of saints, the Scholastics established a program for the transmission of Christ's grace which touched the everyday life of every Christian.

The Scholastic system was holistic. It integrated heaven and earth, God and humanity, justice and mercy—all into the eternal plan of redemption. During this time when the Christian mind was completely preoccupied with the Scholastic system, the Church thought it had found, at last, the perfect means to wholeness and holiness.

THE EMERGENCE OF THE FEMININE

During the period of early Scholastic theology, contemplative prayer was written about as never before. One of the most widely read of contemporary spiritual authors, Abbot John of Fecamp, stressed the sweetness of the spiritual life and emphasized the importance of tears in contemplative prayer. John referred to the inner spirit as "she"—what we would call today the *anima*, or the feminine dimension of human consciousness. For John, contemplative prayer involved openness and receptivity to the indwelling Spirit.

Contemplation—the 'Better Portion'

Spiritual writers frequently stressed the scriptural basis of the life of solitude and contemplative prayer by retelling the story of Martha and Mary (Luke 10:38-41), emphasizing that Mary represents the life of silent, attentive listening to the Lord, while Martha represents the active, busy life of "doing." Mary symbolized for the spiritual writers the feminine virtues of patience and receptivity, while Martha represented the masculine trait of assertive activity by which one seeks to mold the environment to fit one's needs.

In contrast to Martha (symbolizing the *animus* within us), Mary (symbolizing the *anima*) simply waits attentively for the Lord's initiative. Mary's "better portion"—the contemplative life—was characterized by a Carthusian monk as "the raising up into God of the soul enraptured by the taste of eternal joys."[13] The contemplative Mary tasted the joys of the Lord's presence by waiting *before* him rather than by waiting *on* him. The new contemplatives of the 11th and 12th centuries justified their life-styles in the same way. In doing so, they discovered that the human spirit is essentially feminine before God.

The Feminine Dimension

This feminine aspect of spirituality influenced the desire by Western Christians to redefine faith as a relationship rather than purely as assent to doctrine. Abbot Rupert of Cologne (d. 1129) typified monks of his generation when he wrote of the life of faith as "delectable," as "the touch of God" and the "visit of God" in which one "experiences"

God's presence as a loving embrace. The medieval mind became enraptured with its new awareness of God's "sweetness" and "tenderness."

It was an age which strived for *sensibility*, a refined awareness of the emotional content to life and of the necessity for openness to God's initiative in prayer. As new communities of nuns proliferated, female spiritual writers began to appear for the first time.* The anonymous female author of the *Speculum* (12th century) was the first writer to present the spiritual life from the feminine perspective, and at the same time to engage in the cause of a proto-feminism when she reminded her male readers that men and women were children of the same Father and equal in his eyes.

The first woman contemplative about whom we know very much was Abbess Hildegarde of Hesse (1098-1179). Hildegarde was renowned for her visions, and bishops and priests all over Germany sought her counsel—something that would have been unthinkable two centuries earlier. Hildegarde spoke of contemplation as opening the windows of faith, whereby one could experience the Lord in love.

Paradoxically, along with the growth of Marian devotions and a more feminine spirituality, one finds at the same time many male spiritual writers speaking of women in the most degrading of terms. John Chrysostom (347-407) had set a tone in the early Church when he spoke of women as "a domestic peril, a deadly fascination, a painted ill." At the other end of the medieval time span, Thomas Aquinas said that "woman is in subjection according to the law of nature, but a slave is not." In between these two views we find much that is crudely negative. It seems that many medieval men could relate to an idealized paragon such as Mary, but were frightened by the very thought of relating to an actual woman.

Cistercian Spirituality

Because of the rejuvenation of the contemplative life at this time, Christians came to look upon monasticism as "the life of the angels," "the royal way," the "noviceship of eternity" in which Christ was "the abbot of abbots." Thus, the idea still lingered that only monks could truly live the Christian life. Lay people who lived holy lives were really thought to be living a "hidden faithfulness to the monastic profession."[14] Bernard of Clairvaux (1090-1153) brought the monastic ideal to its

---

* Because there is virtually nothing written by women contemplatives before the 12th century, we cannot be confident about the role of early medieval convents in the development of contemplative spirituality.

pinnacle through his new Cistercian spirituality.

In 1098 Robert of Molesme had started a monastic foundation at Citeaux in France. Dedicated to a strict devotion to the Rule of St. Benedict, Robert and his followers believed this Rule had been diluted by the Benedictines of their day. In 1112 the young Bernard joined Robert's foundation, and in 1115 he became abbot of a foundation house at Clairvaux. From Clairvaux, Bernard served as the spiritual father of an entire age. Because of Bernard's leadership, the Cistercian Order grew to 530 monasteries by the end of the 12th century.

Bernard wrote about every conceivable religious topic, but the starting point for both his theology and spirituality was the Bible. A contemporary described his entire life as a "lived experience of the Bible."

Bernard defined spiritual life as "a return to God." Humanity's sinful condition, Bernard said, was caused by the illusion of self, and Bernard constructed for his monks a regimen in which they overcame the self and rose to an awareness of God's presence in their souls. Bernard's starting point for growth from self to God was humility, defined as "a most true knowledge of self by which man becomes lowly in his own sight."[15] Through humility one learns how to restore within oneself the image of God.

Bernard spoke of three "stages" of the spiritual life: (1) unbridled free will, (2) a state in which it is possible not to sin and (3) a state in which it is impossible to sin (achieved only in heaven). The goal of the monk is to surrender his free will through obedience, love and humility and thus ascend to the second stage, where he is gradually transformed into the likeness of God. The spiritual life for Bernard was a continual movement toward more and more wholeness, in which one peels away, as it were, the layers of illusion which hide the self from God.

Unlike Byzantine spirituality during the same period, Western spirituality did not develop "methods" of contemplation. The closest thing to a method in the West was Bernard's teaching on the "remembrance and imitation" of Christ through meditation on Scripture. This affected all future Cistercian spirituality. Two other Cistercians in particular, William of St. Thierry (d. 1148) and Aelred of Rievaulx (d. 1167), further developed Bernard's spirituality.

William, for example, spoke of obedience to the Word of God as the path to spiritual perfection. Through the inner journey of contemplative meditation on Scripture, one moves toward the Spirit, who brings one into the very life of the Trinity, so that the soul becomes not simply "with God" but "like unto God." The power which accomplishes this transformation from self to God is faith, defined as a creative power of interior transformation given to humanity by the Spirit. Like William, Aelred also spoke of the "inner journey" by which one leaves behind the self and moves to God. Sin for William was the "land of unlikeness," from which one seeks escape so that through Christ one may be made "like to God."

Cistercian spirituality captured the feminine energy of the day by stressing the interior life as "Mary"—that is, as patient and obedient receptivity to the Lord's initiative of love. This model of spirituality sought to make Christians whole through the integration within their personalities of *animus* and *anima*, through Martha's doing and Mary's being, through the male characteristic of searching and the female characteristic of receptive waiting. It was a spirituality that was to affect men and women throughout the Middle Ages and into modern times.

A 20th-century spokesman for Bernard, Thomas Merton, summarized the synthetic quality of Cistercian spirituality when he wrote, "The purpose of a monastery is to make men lovers." It is significant that to this day Cistercian monks receive both a male and a female name when they enter monastic life—a masculine name preceded by the name Mary—a telling symbol of the wholeness for which they strive.

CHAPTER SEVEN

TURMOIL AND TRANSITION IN THE HIGH MIDDLE AGES

From the Crusades to the Babylonian Captivity (1095-1305)

In any historical discussion it is always difficult to evaluate the relative influence of thought and events on the shape of the times. Does thought contribute more to events, or do events establish an environment which contributes to certain types of thinking?

Answers to such questions are especially difficult to ascertain in the era known as the High Middle Ages—which is comprised, roughly speaking, of the 12th and 13th centuries. Perhaps never before in history had the ideal of an integrated society—one in which politics, culture, theology and spirituality all come together into a rational, all-embracing system—so affected the lives of human beings.

This was an age in which the ideal of Catholic Christendom—of a world run by Christian principles—reached its fruition. The quest for wholeness, the thrust to bring every impulse of life under the domination of a universally applicable and homogeneous Christian system, reached its zenith in these years—and after these years was never to be hoped for or perhaps even desired again.

Yet during these centuries when the ideal of a unified and universal Christendom most stirred the human imagination, seeds of discord and breakdown were already being sown. In many ways the quest for wholeness epitomized in the events of these centuries was little more than a quest for the unattainable. The literature of the day depicted this unreachable goal in such legends as the quest for the Holy Grail, a sacred object such as Parzival's precious stone, which no one could truly find and possess.

The High Middle Ages, while representing the golden era of the quest for Christian wholeness, would issue forth in tragedy. Not wholeness but the most disastrous disunity characterized the last years of the Christian Middle Ages. But before we reach those latter years, we will trace in this chapter the events of the High Middle Ages and their interplay with spirituality. In the next chapter we will turn to the theology of the High Middle Ages.

THE CRUSADES

The Crusades were a two-century-long war for control of the first Christians' homelands—in particular, Palestine (the "Holy Land"), parts of western Syria and eastern portions of the Byzantine Empire under Moslem domination. As Christian warriors went off to fight the infidels wearing the insignia of the cross—in Spanish, *cruzada*, "marked with the cross"—they came to be known as crusaders.

The Seljuk Threat
Under the Fatimid dynasty (969-1171), the Moslems had been reasonably tolerant of both Christians and Jews living in the Holy Land. But that situation changed when Seljuk Turks—bellicose, nomadic tribes of Moslem warriors—ousted the Fatimids from Jerusalem in 1070. The Seljuks proved to be intolerant of the Christians, and Christian refugees fleeing westward carried with them tales of horrible persecutions.

At this same time the Byzantine Empire, having sustained nearly constant attacks by one Moslem dynasty after another, seemed on the verge of annihilation. This prospect frightened Westerners who, although they doubted the Byzantines' orthodoxy, nonetheless much preferred them as neighbors on their eastern flank than Moslems. Mercantile cities such as Venice and Genoa also worried that a Moslem reconquest of Sicily and Spain would end their monopoly of Mediterranean trade.

So when the Byzantine Emperor Alexius I sent envoys to Pope Urban II seeking Western military support for Byzantium's ongoing war with the Turks, Urban responded favorably and quickly. The pope was no doubt motivated as much by the desire to regain papal prestige in the Christian East as by the desire to recapture the Holy Land. At any rate, he traveled throughout Italy and southern France calling on Christians to travel east to defeat "the accursed race...the unclean nations," as he called the Moslems. When Urban promised a plenary indulgence to all those who accepted his summons to fight, his audiences passionately responded, "God wills it," and tramped off to the East.

The First Crusade
The First Crusade (1095-1099; see map, p. 90) began when some 20,000 idealistic but totally ill-prepared peasants set forth under the leadership of a handful of opportunistic knights. They murdered Jews in the cities of Europe, ran out of money and food, raped and pillaged their way to Constantinople and, on arriving there, looted the churches and homes of their fellow Christians. When they reached Seljuk-controlled Nicaea, they were slaughtered like sheep.

Following behind this mob was an army numbering perhaps 30,000 led by several French nobles (no kings joined the First Crusade). More successful than their pathetic vanguard, these troops made it all the way to Jerusalem (1099) where they stormed the city; ruthlessly murdered nearly 70,000 men, women and children; and for good measure burned the city's Jews alive in their synagogue. The Western nobles divided the conquered territory into four principalities: Jerusalem, Antioch, Edessa and Tripoli. They then elected four from among their ranks as kings.

The Second Crusade
Meanwhile, the Moslems' own preachers urged the various Moslem factions to unite against the invasion of the Christian infidels. The coordinated military effort of the reinspired Moslems—now collectively called by the Latins *Saracens* (from the Arabic *sharqiyun*, or "easterners")—resulted in the Moslem recapture of Edessa in 1144.

Faced with the prospect of a renewed Moslem onslaught, Bernard of Clairvaux and the French King Louis VII (1137-1180) called for a second Crusade. This time two kings, Louis and the German Emperor Conrad III, led the Christian forces east. They were defeated at Damascus in 1148 and, thoroughly disgraced, returned home.

The news of the Christian defeat shocked the West; for the first time Christians began to question the supremacy of their faith. How, they wondered, could soldiers fighting for the one, true faith not prevail against godless infidels? Bernard of Clairvaux's answer—that God allowed the defeat as chastisement for sin—did not satisfy everyone.

The debacle of the Second Crusade, coupled with the growth of an independent spirit of inquiry within the new universities of Europe, inspired many Christian intellectuals to reexamine the faith. They also expanded the confines of theological speculation by inquiring into Arabic and Greek manuscripts now flowing westward (more on this in Chapter Eight).

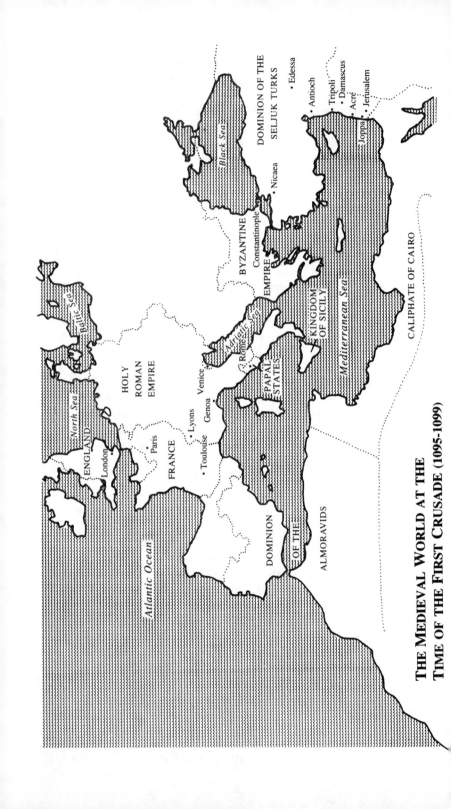

THE MEDIEVAL WORLD AT THE TIME OF THE FIRST CRUSADE (1095-1099)

The Third Crusade

After 40 years of peace, the crusading fever gripped three new kings: Emperor Frederick I (Barbarossa) of Germany, Richard I (the Lionhearted) of England and Philip II Augustus of France. In this Third Crusade Barbarossa drowned on his way east and Philip Augustus returned home after the Christian conquest of Acre (Ah-kray) in 1191. This left Richard the Lionhearted in sole command. Now began a seesaw series of campaigns between Richard and the new Moslem caliph, Saladin. The latter proved to be a tolerant and humane despot who was willing to coexist with Christians in the Holy Land.

When Richard beheaded 2,500 Moslem prisoners in Acre, however, Saladin responded by killing all of his English prisoners. In the ensuing battles the two rulers came to admire and respect each other greatly. Outdoing Western chivalry, Saladin once sent Richard a fresh horse during the height of a pitched battle so that the king could fight with his Moslem adversaries on equal terms. In 1192, having fought each other to exhaustion, the two sides signed a peace treaty which left Richard in control of a coastal stretch of land running from Acre to Joppa, but Saladin in control of Jerusalem. Moslems and Christians were to be protected and tolerated in the other's territory.

The Fourth Crusade

Moslem control of Jerusalem was a bone in the throat for Pope Innocent III (1198-1216), about whom we shall say more shortly. Innocent called for a fourth Crusade. His desire to establish a supranational Christendom under papal leadership, however, deterred the kings of Europe from participating. Thus the Fourth Crusade turned out to be a purely mercenary venture financed by the wealthy city-state of Venice and led by four French nobles lusting after Byzantine treasure. When the crusaders' true intentions were revealed—the sack of Constantinople—Innocent threatened to excommunicate any crusade leader who attacked the Byzantine capital.

Undaunted, the Latin nobles unleashed on Constantinople a furious assault in which their mercenaries sacked the city's churches, libraries and palaces, and raped and murdered virtually at will. Count Baldwin of Flanders emerged as king of the new Latin Kingdom of Constantinople, which governed the city from 1204 to 1261. The Byzantine emperors were forced to move their court to Nicaea until they could drive out the hated Latins.

The so-called Fourth Crusade utterly discredited the crusading movement, brought disgrace upon the papacy, destroyed forever the prospects of a reconciliation between Eastern and Western Churches, and made it easier for the Moslems to consolidate their hold on the East.

The Consequences of the Crusades

Four more disastrous Crusades resulted in the utter collapse of Christian influence in the Holy Land and the establishment of the Moslems as the supreme power in the East. The Crusades had accomplished precisely the opposite effect initially intended. After 1291 the Malmuk dynasty controlled Jerusalem ruthlessly (and wisely) with no thought of tolerance for Christians. In the minds of many Westerners Islam had demonstrated its complete superiority to Christianity.

The general effect of the Crusades on Western society was devastating. Feudalism as a system of social organization was dealt a severe blow. Knights and serfs alike had deserted their lords, either to be killed in the East or to return with no intention of reentering the feudal pyramid. Many landlords had hocked their holdings to urban financiers to raise money for the trip east, and when they returned home penniless they were unable to redeem their estates. With their vassals' power reduced, kings—especially the French kings—had less fear of their barons, who had now become less of an obstacle to monarchical centralization. Consequently, for the first time Christians in the Middle Ages began to develop a national consciousness as opposed to a mentality limited by the demands of their immediate feudal overlord.

From the East a torrent of new thoughts, customs and inventions flooded Western society. The net effect of these alien innovations was to loosen the grip of the faith on the hearts and minds of Christians everywhere. No longer was Christianity an unchallenged belief system. It now had to compete for acceptance.

The institutional Church was perhaps the greatest loser of the Crusades. After popes and preachers had promised victory over the infidel, the crusaders' defeat dealt a blow to the Church's credibility. The Church also suffered another crisis of trust: To finance the Crusades the papal agents had sold indulgences to crusading warriors—often using the money not for the Crusades but for their own struggles with kings and emperors. A contemporary historian, Matthew Paris, observed that many Christians were scandalized to find their donations being used to finance papal military ventures against their own countrymen. Thus was laid the groundwork for the scandal which sparked Luther's revolt two centuries later.

As Christian faith declined in response both to the Islamic victory and to papal and clerical greed, the secularization of medieval society grew commensurately. Commerce, industry and trade all benefited from the Crusades. The merchants of Italy swapped their hatred of Moslem religion for love of Moslem gold. The produce of the East—silk, spices, fruit trees, rugs, glass and all the technology developed by a sophisticated Arabic science—engendered Western taste for things oriental.

At the start of the Crusades, Europe was dominated by feudalism, unquestioning acceptance of the Catholic faith and an economy based solely on agriculture and the ownership of land. At the end, feudalism was in decline, skepticism rivaled faith in the halls of universities, and city-dwelling merchants and financiers threatened to replace the landed gentry as leaders of Western society.

THE AGE OF INNOCENT III

The medieval quest for wholeness was dealt a severe blow during the Crusades, but not a death blow—owing in large part to the efforts by the greatest of medieval popes to bring all of Christian Europe under the sway of his spiritual authority.

The medieval papacy reached the height of its prestige and influence under Pope Innocent III (1198-1216). Innocent had studied theology at Paris and canon law at the University of Bologna. He was at once a deeply spiritual and highly erudite man who based his papacy on proclamation of the gospel and inculcation of the sacramental system. In a papal administration which had become increasingly legalistic in its method of operation, Innocent tried to infuse a spirit of love.

Realizing that the Church badly needed reform, Innocent poured all of his energies into solidifying the work begun by Pope Gregory VII. Innocent attacked the abuses of celibacy and sought to eradicate simony once and for all, failing on both counts. He did manage, however, to restore order and discipline within his own Papal States and to protect the temporal power of the papacy from the threats of the German emperor. He encouraged the crusade ideal by promoting the Fourth and Fifth Crusades to the Holy Land.

Innocent vs. Secular Rulers

Under Innocent the doctrine of papal primacy received a stunning revitalization. The concept of a supranational Christendom—a world dominated by the gospel and governed by the pope—came as close to practical realization as it ever would.

In the Papal States, a wide strip of land running east and west across central Italy, Innocent ruled as a temporal monarch no different from any other king. He hoped to add to his temporal authority the submission of the kings of his day to his spiritual authority.

When Emperor Otto IV (1198-1215) of Germany attacked the Kingdom of Sicily, Innocent acted without hesitation in excommunicating Otto and securing the election of King Frederick of Sicily as king of Germany. (Frederick was grandson of Frederick Barbarossa and was raised in Sicily by his Sicilian mother.)

Innocent's influence was so great that he persuaded many of Otto's German barons to defect from Otto and support Frederick who, as a result, did become emperor—Emperor Frederick II (1215-1250), the greatest king of the Hohenstaufen dynasty. Contrary to Innocent's expectations, Frederick would become an implacable foe of papal authority during the reign of Innocent's successors.

In England, Innocent rejected King John's appointment of the archbishop of Canterbury and imposed on John his own candidate, Stephen Langton. When John resisted and expelled Langton, Innocent imposed an interdict on England (that is, he forbade administration of the sacraments to all English Christians) and then excommunicated the king when the latter seized the property of the English clergy. Popular hostility to the royal usurpation of ecclesiastical authority forced John to relent. John recognized Langton as archbishop and even placed his entire kingdom under the pope's protection as the pope's vassal state.

Later, after John's rebellious vassal-lords forced the king to sign the Magna Carta, John reneged and appealed to Innocent for help. Innocent excommunicated the barons and laid an interdict on London.

In France, Innocent excommunicated King Philip II for divorcing his wife, Queen Ingeborg of Denmark. Like John, Philip was forced by popular sentiment to reconcile with the pope. Thus did Innocent extend the papacy's spiritual authority throughout Europe.

Innocent and Church Reform

Innocent relentlessly sought to reform abuses within the clergy. His guiding principle was his belief that, as he put it, "a shepherd who is unwilling to rebuke those who do wrong leads them to death by his silence." In his many pastoral letters urging reform he painted a sordid picture of clerical life: greed, the abandonment of celibacy, drunkenness, gambling and the pursuit of a comfortable and luxurious life-style.

Innocent's reforming efforts extended to his own Curia, where he curtailed the practice of curial officials accepting bribes for rendering favorable decisions to contestants in ecclesiastical courts. The pope also required bishops throughout Europe to come to Rome every four years in order to make a report to him, thereby personally supervising affairs in their dioceses.

The Albigensian Crusade

One of Innocent's greatest challenges as pope was attempting to eradicate a heretical movement eventually known as Albigensianism.

Starting in the early 12th century, an anti-clerical spirit had manifested itself in southern France, principally in reaction to growing clerical wealth and corruption. A monk named Henry of Lausanne, for example, left his monastery to become a wandering preacher, exhorting the laity to shun the worldly life practiced by the clergy and to take up the simple life-style of the first Christians. Henry denied the objective efficacy of the sacraments, insisting that sacramental validity depended on the sanctity of the sacramental minister.

He attracted quite a following, and some of his supporters sought to force their views on the clergy by desecrating churches and beating and torturing priests. Arnold of Brescia, an Italian priest, likewise took up the cause of clerical reform and likewise taught that a priest's immorality destroyed his power to administer valid sacraments. Arnold had many supporters in Italy until he was put to death on the orders of Frederick Barbarossa.

The increasing call for clerical reform and the demand for the Church to return to apostolic poverty culminated in a movement started by a merchant from the French city of Lyons, Peter Waldo. Around the year 1175 Peter organized a group of lay preachers to go forth exhorting clergy and laity alike to abjure wealth and power and to take on a life of apostolic poverty. Pope Alexander III (1159-1181) had praised the zeal of these "Waldensians" but forbade them from preaching unless supervised by local clergy. The Waldensians disobeyed and stepped up their attacks on the clergy's wealth and its involvement in secular politics.

Gradually the Waldensians came under the influence of a Gnostic group known as the Cathari, who believed in a dualistic creation in which a good god warred with an evil one. For the Cathari, Christ was not the Son of God but an angel who brought a message of enlightenment to the spiritual elite. The mixing of Waldensian beliefs with those of the Cathari became especially prominent in southern France, where the Waldensians began to organize a competing Church by ordaining their own bishops and priests.

Because of the rapid proliferation of heresy, Pope Alexander III sanctioned the use of force against the Waldensians and the Cathari. Hence began an institution known as the *Inquisition*, a judicial procedure by which a person's orthodoxy was challenged. Pope Alexander did not establish a *papal* inquisition, but simply authorized local bishops to conduct their own inquisitions. Eventually these bishops reached the conclusion that the roots of heresy ran so deeply that only violence could extirpate them.

As a result, bishops turned convicted heretics over to local princes for punishment. The latter not only tortured the heretics, but increasingly burned them at the stake. Although such measures temporarily quelled heresy, they weakened the prestige of the Church's hierarchy in the eyes of the lower classes and created a seedbed of smoldering dissent which erupted again into violence in future years.

In Pope Innocent's day the Waldensians and Cathari became especially prominent around the southern French city of Albi and thus became known as *Albigensians*. They rejected the sacraments and belief in hell and purgatory, taught that Christ had been an angel, and organized themselves into communes which rejected private property. Albigensianism was thus simply resurrected Gnosticism, which the early Church had long ago condemned (see *The People of the Creed*, p. 37).

Pope Innocent III felt at first that the Church could defeat the Albigensians simply by steadfastly preaching the gospel and by reforming the clergy's life-style. When reforms and preaching had little effect, however, and when Count Raymond VI of Toulouse refused to punish heretics convicted by local inquisitions, Innocent requested that King Philip II of France undertake a full-scale military crusade against the heretics. The king declined, but a leading French baron, Simon de Montfort, offered to come to the Church's rescue.

Fearing competition from Simon in his own land, Count Raymond of Toulouse then reversed himself, conducting a horrible pogrom against the Albigensians. As just one example, Raymond's soldiers in 1209 murdered over 7,000 elderly people, women and children in the city of Beziers. Such measures shook Pope Innocent badly, and he urged his legates in France to try at all costs to effect a peaceful reconciliation with the heretics.

Innocent's policy was partly successful; several groups of heretics returned to the Church after a series of meetings with Innocent's legates. Innocent received them back into the Church with the most conciliatory gestures. Nonetheless, Raymond's crusaders had done irreparable damage, and the heretical movement outlived Innocent and continued to spread well into the next century (as chronicled by Umberto Eco in his popular novel, *The Name of the Rose*).

FRANCIS AND DOMINIC

Something of monasticism died with Bernard of Clairvaux in 1153. Both Cistercians and Benedictines suffered a spiritual decline during the era of Innocent III, and many of their monasteries relapsed into a worldliness that contradicted the spirit of Benedict's Rule. The monasteries' wealth underlay much of the Albigensian thrust toward poverty we have just considered. Yet many faithful Christians truly desired to practice the gospel ideal of poverty within the confines of the Catholic Church.

Both Francis Bernardone (1181-1226) and Dominic Guzman (1170-1221) were able to harness this healthy aspect of the growing desire for evangelical poverty and point it in a new direction—away from both heresy and monasticism and toward an entirely new Christian life-style known as *mendicancy*, which literally means "begging."

The new mendicant orders, the Franciscans and the Dominicans, combined the monastic virtues of poverty, chastity and obedience with the active life-style of the secular clergy. Thus the mendicants—who called themselves "friars" rather than monks—did not confine themselves to a life of monastic solitude but traveled from place to place preaching the gospel and depending on alms for their daily existence.

Mendicancy and Lay Spirituality

Mendicancy must be seen against the background of an indigenous lay spirituality which had begun to develop during the 12th century. The Dominicans and Franciscans were not innovators so much as they were systematizers of an impulse toward the mendicant life-style which predated the births of Dominic and Francis.

With the growth of cities and universities, and the rise of mercantile and financial classes, many more people could now read and think for themselves than in the heyday of feudalism. In the cities it was not as hard to locate a Bible as on feudal manors, and so the new class of literate laypersons began to read the Bible for themselves. In addition, with their minds sharpened by finance and business, they began to speculate on the meaning of the Scriptures heard at Mass.

Christians naturally started comparing the simple life-style of Jesus and his apostles with the luxuriant life-style of their clergy—often discrediting the latter in comparison to the former. Some lay Christians began to take the Gospels as the only norm of Christian conduct. As a result, they sought to pattern their lives less on the example set for them by the institutional hierarchy than on the simplicity of the first Christians.

In addition, various spiritual writers of the day stressed the centrality of the Gospels and their emphasis on the equality of all Christians. For example, one writer made a reference to the equality of all believers when he said, "Rich and poor, noble and serf, merchant and peasant, all and every one who professes himself a Christian must cast away everything inimical to that name, and follow what is conformable to it."[1]

Another writer echoed this sentiment by saying, "If anyone asks what is your religious profession, your rule, your order, answer that it is the first and principal rule of the whole Christian religion: the gospel, the source and principle of all the others."[2] And again, "We consider as Regulars [clergy] not only those who renounce the world and enter religion, but all the faithful of Christ who served the Lord under the gospel and under the supreme abbot [Christ]."[3]

The Institutionalization of the Friars

This egalitarian gospel shocked clergy and nobles alike. While many Christians recognized the new Franciscan and Dominican orders as the healthy flowering of seed already planted among the laity, others—principally among the hierarchy of the Church and the nobility—saw both the new lay spirituality and the mendicant orders as a subtle form of revolution in which lower-class usurpers threatened the privileges of the wealthy and powerful.

Both prelates and nobles thus attempted to dilute the mendicants' simple preaching by binding the Franciscans and Dominicans to strict institutional control. Through such measures lay people would either have to join a mendicant order stripped of its fervor, or remain as lay people and run the risk of being labeled as heretics for espousing beliefs which could easily be made to appear as Albigensian. Thus, it was hoped, the principal means by which the laity could express its desire to live in evangelical poverty would be eliminated. Then, it was also hoped, the new lay spirituality would disappear.

Consequently, what Dominic and Francis had started as a spontaneous gospel life-style dedicated to poverty and preaching became more institutionalized. Dominic's preachers—whom he had sent forth, as he put it, "Like doves to combat the vipers of Heresy"—gradually became highly educated men. By Dominic's death in 1221 his preachers were becoming the special advisers of popes and great doctors of theology in major universities.

Likewise—almost in purposeful contradiction to their simple founder's life-style—the Franciscans became scholars and teachers at great universities such as Oxford and Paris. The future course of Scholastic theology was largely dependent upon the work of Dominicans and Franciscans, something that neither Dominic nor Francis would have foreseen.

This shift in emphasis from the humble life-style of beggars and preachers to highly organized orders of scholars led to quarrels among the mendicants themselves. Quarrels among the Franciscans led some to return to the primitive simplicity of their origins as "Spiritual Franciscans" in contrast to the increasingly institutionalized "Regular Franciscans." (It is this conflict which is the backdrop to Eco's *The Name of the Rose*. For those who persevere I will translate and explain the cryptic last line of this novel in an upcoming chapter.)

The Church Tries Violence

In a development which would have perhaps shocked Francis and Dominic, the papacy gradually began to use Dominicans and Franciscans as *inquisitors* (prosecutors of the Inquisition). The Church's fight against heresy had never abated—even with the severity of the Albigensian Crusade. All over Europe anti-clerical, Albigensian-like groups proliferated, dedicated to Gnostic ideals of communism, the abolition of Christian morality and authority, and the establishment of an unstructured society in which priests and nobles would be eliminated.

Such groups—motivated by goals of social as well as religious revolution—posed a real threat to the faith, whether considered as objective Church doctrine or as relationship with Christ. (The neo-Gnostics repeatedly denied Christ's divinity and salvific mission.) In response to this burgeoning threat to the faith, the Church reacted—or overreacted—violently.

The policy of Archbishop Albert of Magdeburg in eastern Germany epitomized the depths to which some bishops felt compelled to stoop:

> Anyone who has been convicted of heresy by the bishop of his diocese must immediately, upon the bishop's demand, be arrested by the secular judicial authority and delivered up to the pyre. Should the judges mercifully spare his life, he must at least suffer the loss of his tongue, by which the Catholic faith has been assailed.[4]

Such measures, of course, only weakened the faith. Further, in addition to the traditional local episcopal inquisitions, there was now a new development. Pope Gregory IX (1227-1241) instituted the office of *papal inquisitor*, thus establishing a permanent office within the Curia for the systematic eradication of heresy. Beginning about 1232 heretics were increasingly turned over to the Dominicans, who were authorized to proceed by secret trials in which the names of witnesses were withheld from the accused, and representation by lawyers and the right to appeal were forbidden. In a decree dated May 15, 1252, Pope

Innocent IV officially authorized torture as a means of securing evidence and confessions from accused heretics.

Effect on the Mendicants

Despite the transformation of the original conception of mendicant life, the Franciscans and Dominicans together constituted the most important spiritual force of the 13th century. They transformed the Church even as they were transformed by it. Perhaps it was asking too much to expect that a man like Francis—who "rose on the world like the sun," as Dante wrote—could impose forever his simple, unencumbered spirit on a group of men that had grown to some 40,000 by the year 1300.

Some measure of institutionalization was inevitable. Yet it was an ominous portent for the greatest spiritual movement of the day to be brought so swiftly and efficiently into the bureaucracy of the Church, and then to be used as an arm of the Inquisition. Once the institutionalized mendicant orders no longer provided an effective outlet for the expression of the simple gospel life-style, many lay Christians began to question the need for the institutional Church altogether. As we shall see in Chapter Ten, this questioning was to lead to the 14th-century reform movements which, although temporarily squelched, anticipated Luther by a century.

And, as if to hasten the inevitable, the popes after Innocent III seemed to do everything in their power to destroy papal prestige and credibility.

THE BABYLONIAN CAPTIVITY OF THE PAPACY

When Pope Innocent III died in 1216, the Church passed once again into a period dominated by the struggle between papacy and empire. Pope Honorius III (1216-1227), ill throughout his entire papacy, was no match for the new Sicilian-born German emperor, Frederick II, who tried repeatedly to subjugate the papacy and bring it into his sphere of influence.

Under Pope Innocent IV (1243-1254), the papacy freed itself momentarily from the imperial threat. At the Council of Lyons (1245) Innocent secured the deposition of Frederick as emperor and freed Frederick's subjects from their oaths of fealty. Frederick died in 1250. When his last heir, Conradin, died in 1268, the imperial legacy passed to the house of Hapsburg, whose princes left the papacy unbothered during the rest of the 13th century. (The Hapsburgs ruled as crowned heads of various European states until 1918.)

In 1261 a Frenchman, Urban IV, became pope. The Pope and his Curia offered the now-vacant throne of Sicily to the powerful French baron, Charles of Anjou, brother of the French king, Louis IX (St. Louis, 1226-1270). When Urban IV died in 1264, he was succeeded by another Frenchman, Clement IV, who crowned Charles of Anjou King of Sicily. When Clement died, the cardinals could not decide on a new pope for three years, and Charles of Anjou became master of Italy. The papacy had thrown off the yoke of the German emperors only to discover that the French were just as eager to control the Church.

Pope Boniface vs. Nationalism

The iron-willed Pope Boniface VIII (1294-1303) was determined to assert the papacy's ancient primacy against the policies of the King of France. Boniface came from the Roman nobility, had studied law at Bologna and fully intended to return the status of Church-State relations to what they had been under Innocent III — that is, he wanted to assert the supremacy of the papal office over the power of the State at every opportunity.

In 1296 Boniface issued a papal "bull" (a solemn document sealed with a *bulla*, or lead seal, to authenticate it) entitled *Clericis Laicos* (*Clergy and the Laity*) which forbade the clergy to pay taxes to any secular ruler without papal consent. It also threatened with excommunication any secular ruler who received such taxes.

The bull was directed at the policies of King Philip IV ("the Fair") of France and King Edward I of England, both of whom vehemently resisted Boniface's attempts to take away one of their chief sources of revenue. In contrast to the situation in Innocent's day (see p. 94), both kings had the solid support of their subjects. Boniface thus could not enforce his policies as had Innocent III. A new day was dawning in Europe — one dominated by national loyalties rather than by loyalty to the pope.

In England, the Magna Carta (1215) had inspired the nobles to demand a say in government. Under King Edward I, parliament started to become the source of both civil law and anti-papal nationalist pride. Although the English bishops served in Edward's "Model Parliament" of 1295, they could not prevent the gradual secularization of English law. Lords and commoners alike stripped the English Church of its many privileges — a process which would culminate in the English Reformation under Henry VIII.

In France, a king and saint, Louis IX, steadily increased the power and prestige of the French crown, making France the greatest state in Europe. In 1286, St. Louis asserted the independence of the

French Church by prohibiting papal appointments of bishops and Church taxation without the prior consent of the crown and French bishops. Thus was born French "Gallicanism," the independence of the French Catholic Church from Rome.

All over Europe Christians began to regard themselves as citizens of a nation-state first and of a universal Christendom second. "We are Venetians; after that we are Christian" was the motto of Venice and, in effect, that of all the other independent city-states of Italy, the very bastion of papal influence. Only a half-century after his death, Innocent III had been denied his dream of establishing a united Christendom under papal leadership. The spirit of the times was nationalistic and not Catholic.

The Victory of National Sovereignty

King Philip IV, in keeping with the spirit of the times, circulated a series of pamphlets such as *A Dialogue Between a Cleric and a Knight*, which advanced the proposition that a national Church was bound to support the king as the Church's divinely ordained protector. Pope Boniface VIII responded with another bull in 1302, *Ausculta Fili* (*Listen, Son!*), in which he proclaimed the absolute supremacy of pope over king.

When King Philip forbade publication of this bull in France, Boniface published another, *Unam Sanctam* (*One, Holy*), in which he declared that there was "One Holy, Catholic, and Apostolic Church," outside of which "neither salvation nor the remission of sins" was possible.

Further, the bull said, to disobey the pope was to exclude oneself from the Church. Both the "temporal sword" and the "spiritual sword" had been given by God to the pope, and thus the papacy had been divinely instituted as superior to the monarchy.

Enraged by Boniface's repeated assertions of supremacy, King Philip sent his councillor, Nogaret, to Rome to arrest Boniface and bring him back to France for trial. Nogaret arrested Boniface in his bed, but was forced by Romans loyal to the pope to return to France without him. The pope died of shame and humiliation a few months after the incident.

The papacy which had once proudly asserted its independence from the empire now found itself the captive of a new force — nationalism. The laity in the new nation-states stood behind their kings against the papacy, and thus the spiritual influence of the strong popes of earlier eras meant little or nothing to Christians outside of Italy.

In 1305, the College of Cardinals once again elected a Frenchman, Pope Clement V, who became entirely subservient to King

Philip and his nationalized French Church. In 1309 Clement moved the papal headquarters to Avignon in southeast France, where the popes resided until 1377.

The contemporary Italian poet Francesco Petrarch (1304-1374) referred to the popes' stay in France as the "Babylonian Captivity," an apt metaphor to describe the condition of a papacy which had lost sight of its spiritual mission by becoming overly involved—like Israel of old—with the affairs of the nations.

Impact on the Faith

The effect of the events we have just discussed on the faith of Christians was twofold:

1) On the level of objective doctrine, the Crusades, the upsurge of lay spirituality with its call for evangelical poverty, the Inquisition and violent suppression of heresy—all combined to make the faith much less certain, absolute and immutable.

2) On the level of subjective relationship with Christ, many Christians turned away from liturgical and sacramental forms of devotion, or combined these with new forms of interior contemplation, which made the faith increasingly more personal and less communal—a development which was to have both positive and negative effects, as we shall see (p. 158 ff.). Before continuing this aspect of the story, we turn now to the greatest epoch of medieval theology.

CHAPTER EIGHT

THE FAITH IN RESPONSE TO ARISTOTLE

The Classical Age of Scholasticism—the 13th Century

Three forces contributed to bring the early Scholasticism which we considered in Chapter Six to its summit in the 13th century: (1) the development of universities, (2) the predominance of Dominicans and Franciscans as teachers in these universities and (3) the incorporation of the philosophy of Aristotle into the theology taught at these universities. Taken together, these three factors constituted a revolution in the history of Christian thought.

Universities Set the Stage

During the 12th century the first universities such as Paris, Bologna and Oxford began to take on an identity separate from the cathedral schools out of which they had evolved. Initially, university life was strictly religious and ecclesiastical. The first university students were clerics, and the professors likewise were all members of the clergy. Both the professors and the courses of study had to be approved by the local bishop and, in cases of controversy, by the Roman Curia. Eventually, however, universities began to offer other courses besides theology. The University of Bologna, which very early had schools of law and medicine, led the way.

As a result, a division of the universities into secular and theological "faculties" began to take place. As this process occurred, it became increasingly difficult for universities to maintain their strictly ecclesiastical atmosphere. More and more lay students came to the universities, interested in learning not just theology but also science and the arts, and lay professors began to teach such subjects.

A struggle developed between those who wanted to limit university curricula solely to theology and those who wanted to open the curricula to nontheological disciplines. The battleground upon which this struggle was waged was the philosophy of Aristotle. We can understand neither the future course of Scholasticism nor the future course of Christian thinking in general unless we know at least a little about the Aristotelian philosophy that now began to confront Augustinian neo-Platonism, which for centuries had completely dominated Western theology.

ARISTOTLE AND HIS PHILOSOPHY

Although early medieval scholars had possessed some of Aristotle's treatises on logic, they had not possessed his treatises on science, metaphysics and ethics. As part of the influx of Arabic thought coming to the West after the Crusades, Moslem commentaries on Aristotle—particularly the commentaries by the Moslem scholars Avicenna (d. 1037) and Averroes (d. 1189)—were the first channels through which long-forgotten parts of Aristotle's writings were transmitted to the West.

Aristotle (384-322 B.C.) had idolized his teacher, Plato; he built an altar to his great master when he died. Yet Aristotle could not follow in Plato's philosophical footsteps. Aristotle was a doctor's son, and even while listening to Plato's teaching on preexistent, universal forms (see *The People of the Creed*, p. 26), his mind wandered to the more observable aspects of the physical world.

Plato started from such conceptual premises as God, forms, ideas and the absolute. The foundation of his thought was thus the *a priori* self-existence of the ideal world from which the actual world took its shape. Aristotle started from the opposite direction. He wanted to touch and see and feel truth in material creation, and then reason back to first principles.

Whereas Plato had his students engage in lofty dialogues, Aristotle sent his pupils out into the fields to gather flowers and herbs and seeds and to other lands to learn at first hand practical lessons in politics, ethics and aesthetics. For him the means to knowledge were the five senses. He wanted to construct a theory of the universe not out of his head but from experiment and observation.

We could really call Aristotle a scientist as much as a philosopher. Whereas Plato was the champion of deduction, Aristotle was the father of induction and of the scientific method.

Plato saw all matter as descending from ultimate, absolute spiritual reality, so that the farther material creation devolved from its spiritual source, the less spiritual—the less God-like—it became. Aristotle spoke not of descent but of a "continuous scale of ascent," an evolution *upward* from lifeless objects to the higher forms of life.

For Aristotle, therefore, the soul is a vital principle toward which the "human organism" grows and moves. Although all organisms possess a soul, he said, it is only humanity which possesses the "active rational soul," which he also called "active intellect."

But this active intellect is not personal; that is, it does not survive as a distinct entity after death. Rather, the active intellect is united to the body only during a person's life and continues its own existence after a person dies. The active intellect is the force which motivates all growth. Aristotle called this force the "prime mover unmoved," which he equated with God.

For Aristotle, God is the final end or goal of all growth and evolution. God does not create the world so much as he energizes it, moving it from within as the force which draws all creation to perfection in him. God is consciousness or thought, thinking himself into fruition through the unfolding evolution of material creation. Aristotle explained this process by saying, "Thought thinks itself as object in virtue of its participation in what is thought."

Controversy Arises

Even this smattering of Aristotle's philosophy should indicate to us that Aristotelianism was incompatible with Christianity on certain key points. Aristotle's "active intellect," for example, meant that there was no such thing as personal immortality. The active intellect was a sort of "world soul" common to everyone, thus making the Christian view of individual immortality meaningless. Further, for Aristotle, God was the prime mover but not the *creator* of the world, which Aristotle held to be eternally existent. Taken as a whole, Aristotle's newly discovered philosophy seemed to many Christians a rationalistic threat to supernatural faith.

In 1215 Pope Innocent III's legate to Paris forbade the study of Aristotle's metaphysics and natural philosophy. This caused quite a stir because students all over Europe were by then intoxicated with the new philosophy. When the prohibition against Aristotle's works was extended to the University of Toulouse, the faculty simply ignored the papal ban and taught Aristotle anyway.

One of the major controversies arising from the rediscovery of Aristotle was a debate over the reality of "universals," general concepts representing individuals of the same class. For example, the individuals Mary and John are represented by the universal concept of humanity. Theologians like Anselm, writing in the Augustinian neo-Platonist tradition, believed universals were real—that is, they have a real existence in the mind of God apart from individuals. Anselm and those who thought like him were called Realists, while those who thought that universals were simply names with no real existence apart from individuals were called Nominalists.

Aristotle's philosophy naturally bolstered the Nominalist position, while Plato's supported the Realist position. For the Realists, Aristotle's philosophy meant the destruction of absolute values such as goodness, virtue, beauty, love and the like; the Realists feared that Aristotle's philosophy would lead to the tyranny of the individual.

We will see later (p. 135) how this competition between Realism and Nominalism played itself out in the political sphere. For the moment, we mention this differing view toward universals simply to underscore the sense of anxiety which traditional Augustinian neo-Platonists experienced when Aristotle's philosophy came into vogue.

SCHOLASTIC RESPONSES TO ARISTOTLE

The Scholastic reaction to Aristotle aligned itself into roughly three camps: (1) those who upheld traditional Augustinian theology and sought to submit Aristotle to that theology; (2) those who tried to harmonize the Augustinian tradition with the new Aristotelianism; and (3) those who felt that it was impossible to harmonize Augustine with Aristotle and advocated the unfettered study of Aristotle as a separate academic discipline. The first reaction can be thought of as an attempt to keep theology supreme over philosophy, the second as an attempt to synthesize theology and philosophy, and the third as a belief that theology and philosophy are separate disciplines.

We will look first at this threefold Scholastic reaction to Aristotle, and then we will discuss the effect each type of reaction had on the future course of Christian thinking.

Bonaventure and the Franciscans

The leading supporters of traditional Augustinianism were two Franciscans, Alexander of Hales and Giovanni di Fidanza—whom we know as Bonaventure. Since Alexander's thought was eclipsed by the work of Bonaventure, his most famous student, we will not discuss Alexander in detail. Yet it was he who founded the 13th-century school of Franciscan theology which remained faithful to Augustinianism.

Alexander knew of Aristotle's writings and quoted him often—whenever the philosopher's words tended to support Alexander's *true* authorities, Augustine and Anselm. Alexander's theology was oriented toward spirituality. He did not believe it the business of theologians to build speculative systems of thought about God, but rather to "move the soul toward *the good* through principles of love and fear."[1] ("The good" was a Platonic way of speaking about God.) Thus, the Franciscan theologians felt that theology was the truest path to wisdom, and that a philosophy not submitted to theology could lead to error.

Bonaventure (1221-1274) neither condemned nor rejected Aristotle. But, although he respected Aristotle's scientific studies, he could not accept Aristotle's teaching on God and the soul. For Bonaventure, belief and understanding are two separate activities: Belief is based on revealed authority while understanding is based on reason. Philosophy (the science of reason) was a worthwhile endeavor, Bonaventure thought, but it could never proceed past the frontier of revealed doctrine (faith). Hence, while Aristotle might have some valuable insights, the Christian philosopher must not pursue any study of those aspects of Aristotle which clearly contradict revealed truth. Anyone who goes farther, Bonaventure said, "falls into darkness."

Bonaventure believed in the supremacy of the will over the intellect—that is, he believed that faith is a better path to knowledge of God than intellectual speculation. For Bonaventure, faith as submission to God's revelation is the supreme means of knowledge. He believed that human reason can assist faith only by studying the Trinitarian "imprints" which God has placed in his creation. (This was an Augustinian idea; see *The People of the Creed*, p. 125.) In all created things, Bonaventure said, there are three "vestiges" of the Trinity—being, truth and goodness. These Trinitarian imprints are found in the human faculties of memory, intellect and will, which are the means God has given humanity to ascend toward him.

For Bonaventure, the ascent toward God did not culminate in rational understanding but in mystical contemplation, a state in which intellectual knowledge is superfluous because the soul experiences God as he is in himself and not as philosophy has conceived of him through study. Thus Bonaventure proceeded from faith as objective doctrine to faith as contemplative, mystical relationship. For him, the path to wholeness was guided by the heart and the will rather than the mind and the intellect.

Thomas Aquinas and the Dominicans

Beginning with Albert the Great (1200-1280), Dominican theologians began to take a more liberal approach to the use of Aristotle's works. The Dominicans did not disagree with Bonaventure that Augustine had been the greatest of the Church Fathers. But they went further, seeking a way to incorporate Aristotle into Augustine's system. Or, to put it another way, they wanted to harmonize philosophy and theology, reason and faith.

Albert's intellectual orientation was a lot like Aristotle's. He had a wide-ranging interest in natural science and wrote on such topics as astronomy, botany and zoology. He believed that theology could properly avail itself of the methods and findings of these studies.

The greatest Dominican scholar, and the greatest theologian of the Middle Ages, was Albert's student, Thomas Aquinas (1225-1274). As a philosopher, Thomas became the leading Scholastic commentator on Aristotle. Thus, as a theologian, Thomas was naturally influenced by Aristotle's method. Thomas believed that those who feared Aristotle's natural philosophy and metaphysics were positing a false dichotomy between philosophy and theology, faith and reason.

Whereas Bonaventure believed the *will* provided the surest path to truth (through faith), Thomas Aquinas believed the *intellect* as well as the will could lead one to the truth. In reality, Thomas said, faith and reason—even Aristotle's scientific method—are not in conflict with each other. Rather, they are simply different ways of looking at truth. Philosophy approaches truth strictly through reason, while theology looks at truth "in the light of divine revelation." There is thus no reason to fear "natural knowledge," since it can never exceed the higher form of knowledge, which is faith.

Thomas thus put the new Aristotelianism at the service of faith. For the first time theology went beyond Platonic conceptualizing and began to rely on sensory data as a tool in arriving at its conclusions. Compared to Bonaventure and the entire Augustinian neo-Platonist tradition, Thomas was only a *moderate* Realist—that is, he said that there are no independently existing universals. Rather, he believed that universals such as humanity exist only in individual entities such as the human persons John and Mary.

Thomas also made theology more incarnational; he removed from it the bias of earlier Christian thinkers who had frequently been suspicious of allowing God and humanity, grace and nature, spirit and matter, to come too close together. Thomas brought theology more into contact with the concrete world in which the human Jesus had lived.

Thomas's guiding theological principle was "faith presupposes natural knowledge, just as grace does nature and all perfections that which they perfect."[2] This Thomistic principle was formulated in the maxim "Grace follows nature," meaning that the natural world—far from being inimical to spiritual truth—is the very means by which one attains that truth.

Such thinking was regarded as dangerous in the 13th century, and in 1277 the bishop of Paris condemned certain propositions of Thomas. Franciscan scholars in particular led the assault on Thomas, and when Dominicans rose to Thomas's defense, a state of intellectual warfare broke out between the two orders, not settled until Pope John XXII canonized Thomas Aquinas in 1323. Two centuries later Thomas was accorded the title "Universal Doctor of the Church," and from then on "Thomism" became the basis of all Catholic theology until well into the 20th century.

Siger of Brabant

Thomas Aquinas acknowledged that faith and reason could sometimes *appear* to reach contradictory conclusions. When this happened, Thomas said, there was actually no contradiction since the truths of faith encompassed the truths of natural knowledge and thus, in a sense, outdistanced them. For that reason theology was superior to philosophy even while using philosophy's own method. (Here he agreed with Bonaventure.)

Siger of Brabant (1240-1284), like Thomas a professor at the University of Paris, went a step further. Siger taught that when one reaches conclusions by way of philosophy which appear to contradict the faith, one submits in obedience to the faith but nonetheless acknowledges that there is in fact a contradiction. Thus, unlike Bonaventure, who subordinated philosophy to theology, and unlike Thomas who tried to harmonize the two, Siger in effect said, "Let's be honest with ourselves and admit that philosophy and theology are independent disciplines often going in two opposite directions."

Siger thus taught that philosophy should be independent from theology and not subordinated to it. To most Scholastics this position was erroneous. Eventually, nearly the entirety of Siger's work was condemned.

CONSEQUENCES FOR THE FUTURE

The three reactions to Aristotle discussed above had differing effects on the future course of Christian thought.

The Influence of Siger

Although the influence of Siger and his colleagues waned as a major force within theology by the 14th century, their extreme Aristotelianism continued to make its influence felt, if only negatively. From the time of Siger onward the Church hierarchy became increasingly suspicious of science and philosophy as autonomous disciplines. The hierarchy chose Thomas Aquinas as the only safe route by which "natural studies" could enter into universities and seminaries.

Eventually this attitude became inflexible. During the scientific revolution of the 17th century, for example, the hierarchy would not tolerate an independent science and forced such a reputable and devout Christian scientist as Galileo Galilei to retract his theories. The Church has admitted this error only in our own day.

The hierarchy's exaggerated reaction to Siger and his school established within Christian thought a false dichotomy between religion and science which still influences Christian thinking. As late as the 1950's, Teilhard de Chardin, a French Jesuit and scientist of unquestioned abilities, was censured by his superiors for trying to integrate religion and science through a unified explanation of God's creation.

Through his work Teilhard was simply resuming the quest for integrative wholeness which Thomas Aquinas had pursued. After the Protestant Reformation of the 16th century rejected Thomas's synthesis, there had been no synthetic model for the harmonization of faith and reason until Teilhard. (We will pursue the breakup of the medieval synthesis as achieved by Thomas in *The People of Anguish: The Story Behind the Reformation*, and Teilhard's reestablishment of that synthesis in *The People of Hope: The Story Behind the Modern Church*.)

The Influence of Thomas Aquinas

For Thomas, in studying the things of God, "we make use of his effects, either of nature or of grace," because "grace does not abolish nature but completes it." Thus, "natural reason should minister to faith, just as the natural inclination of the will ministers to the love created by grace."[3]

Thomas's writings stand for the proposition that Christianity is a fully incarnational religion. Just as the eternal Word entered fully into material creation by becoming man, so too does Thomas's theology harmonize spirit and flesh, sensory investigation and abstract speculation, inductive analysis and deductive reasoning.

In the early Church a constant struggle between spirit and matter had been waged by those who feared and mistrusted earthly creation as base and evil (see, for example, *The People of the Creed*, p. 85).

With Thomas this struggle finally comes to an end. In a theology where we find the truth about God in the stuff of which the earth is made, the Church's proclamation that "the Word became flesh and dwelt among us" is logically consistent. In Thomas's system the faith becomes intellectually respectable. In him the Middle Ages' quest for wholeness reaches its highest summit: Faith and reason are united; heaven and earth are drawn together into one consistent system of thought.

Thomas's contribution is beautifully summarized by Umberto Eco in *The Name of the Rose*. The villain of the story is a Platonist monk who kills everyone in his monastery who tries to read a long-lost copy of one of Aristotle's treatises. When the hero, a Franciscan, confronts the murderer, the latter justifies his crimes by saying,

> Every book by that man has destroyed a part of the learning that Christianity had accumulated over the centuries....Before, we used to look to reason, deigning only a frowning glance at the mire of matter; now we look at the earth, and we believe in the heavens because of earthly testimony.

A concise summary of Thomas's achievement by a master storyteller!

In assessing the effect of Thomas Aquinas on the future course of Christian thinking, we become aware of the mixed blessings of genius. Like Augustine before him or, for that matter, like anyone who dominates an age by his surpassing creativity, Thomas placed everyone else in his shadow. That is not to say that he did not have his detractors or challengers or that his work was universally accepted.

Yet, within three centuries Thomas was to become *the* theologian of the Catholic Church. And whereas an exclusive attachment to Platonism had created problems for early Christianity (see *The People of the Creed*, p. 60), so would rigid adherence to Thomism deprive Catholicism of the verve and ingenuity it would need to change with the times.

Thomas himself would have resented this overarching reliance on his writings to the virtual exclusion of other perspectives. It is significant to recount Thomas's own evaluation of his work, which came shortly before his death. After celebrating Mass in December 1272, Thomas terminated his writing because, as he put it, "Such things have been revealed to me that all I have written seems as so much straw."

The Influence of Bonaventure
In evaluating Bonaventure we find a writer whose spirituality

permeates every page of his theology. With the possible exceptions of John Scotus Erigena and Bernard of Clairvaux, we can say that in Bonaventure the Christian West achieved for the first time a mystagogy (see p. 21) to match that of the Byzantines. In Bonaventure medieval Christians' quest for personal wholeness finds an eloquent spokesman.

In the writings of this great Franciscan—the "irrefutable doctor," as he was called—the deepest currents of monastic spirituality were put at the service of theology. Bonaventure kept alive the ever developing Christian impulse to define faith as the direct experience of God. Bonaventure echoes in his works the sentiments of Bernard of Clairvaux who, in preaching to his monks, frequently started with such words as, "We shall read today in the book of experience. Turn your minds inward upon yourselves...."[4]

Bonaventure thought in the same vein as did the mystic Richard of St. Victor (d. 1173) who wrote of the superiority of the "book of experience" over all study, and of the need for "the light of illumining grace" to lead one "to penetrate profound mysteries by the inspiration of grace."[5]

The starting point for Bonaventure's spirituality was introspection on the images of Scripture where, as Bonaventure put it, "we enter ourself, that is, our own mind, in which is reflected God's very own image."[6] From this perspective of the "inner world," one "sees God in the splendor of the saints";[7] one is "transported in ecstasy above the intellect"[8] to deep awareness of God as he is in himself, and not necessarily as he is in theology texts.

So certain was Bonaventure of the necessity of this mystical dimension to Christian spirituality that he placed it on the same level as participation in the sacraments, which should be administered, Bonaventure wrote, only to those who "first descend by grace, into their own heart."[9] Bonaventure's model of the Christian mystic was "our most blessed father Francis" who, Bonaventure said, on numerous occasions had been "transported out of himself," becoming "a model of perfect contemplation"[10] for every Christian.

Bonaventure's writings stand for the proposition that the sacramental system is deficient if it is not based on development of the inner person through contemplative prayer. Bonaventure did not say that without contemplative prayer the sacraments are inefficacious, but he did believe that one could not fully experience the worth of the sacraments without such prayer.

As we shall see in the next chapter, Bonaventure's perspective would become further enriched by the increasing tendency toward mysticism in the spirituality of the 14th and 15th centuries.

The Protestant Reformation of the 16th century resulted, in a sense, from Catholicism's inadequate response to Bonaventure. His conception of the faith as personal relationship with God through contemplative prayer was offset by a too mechanistic and ritualistic understanding of the faith on the part of many Catholics.

Yet future Catholic mystics such as Ignatius of Loyola, Teresa of Avila and John of the Cross would keep alive Bonaventure's subjectivism, so that the medieval understanding of contemplative prayer would never die out in the Catholic tradition.

CHAPTER NINE

OF SAINTS AND SINNERS

Everyday Faith During the Middle Ages

Not everyone in the Middle Ages was a Thomas Aquinas, interested in intellectual pursuits. Nor was every Christian a Francis of Assisi, drawn to the mendicant life-style. It would be as much of a distortion to pass off such luminaries as Thomas Aquinas and Francis of Assisi as "typical" medieval Christians as to say that all 20th-century Christians have the zeal of Mother Teresa or the insights of Karl Rahner.

As in our own day, so in the Middle Ages, the average Christian had "average" concerns—family problems, making a living, trying to make the gospel a reality amid the many distractions of workaday existence. Christians in the Middle Ages, like Christians today, had their own style of practicing the faith in order to find support for struggling with these everyday concerns.

We could define this attempt by the ordinary believer to place his or her unique stamp upon formal theology and spirituality as "everyday faith." If theology and spirituality as we have studied it thus far could be called the ideal of medieval Christianity, then everyday faith could be called the actuality. Sometimes the ideal and the actuality coalesced, but many times they did not. Yet everyday faith—even when it stretched the limits of orthodox theology and spirituality to the breaking point—greatly influenced the future direction of Christian thought and belief.

One could make a strong argument for this proposition: Medieval everyday faith has exerted greater influence upon modern Christianity than anything written by theologians. Whereas theology must be learned and acquired, everyday faith is something affecting one as deeply and spontaneously as language, nationality or race. In studying the everyday faith we are getting at the deepest sentiments of what individuals think and believe. And people are not nearly as threatened by assaults on the intellectual foundation of their faith as they are by attempts to dissuade them from doing what comes naturally.

Let's take a simple example. Most Christians have learned that folding their hands together with fingers pointed upward is a gesture which signifies prayer. When someone tells us that this custom comes from the pagan Germanic ritual by which a vassal pledged loyalty to his lord—by inserting both hands within his lord's hands—we could perhaps think, "How interesting." Yet if someone came into the typical church next Sunday and said, "Today we will all begin to pray with outstretched palms as the early Christians did," most likely the congregation would rather fight than switch.

Everyday faith is like this. It has a deep hold on a person's psyche—much deeper than anything one can explain through rational discourse. Thus it is very difficult for the historian to define precisely the influence that "official" doctrine had on the medieval mind.

In fact, it is possible that the historian of religion goes in the wrong direction by poring over the writings of intellectuals. The historian would perhaps better spend time pondering why people genuflect before entering their pews or why they cross themselves with holy water when leaving church. No one today cares whether it was Aquinas or Bonaventure who responded better to Aristotle, but just watch an otherwise dreary congregation come to life when it starts to vocalize "Immaculate Mary, your praises we sing."

THE CULT OF THE SAINTS

Now that we have some idea of what is meant by "everyday faith," let's take a brief look at certain essential characteristics of this faith during the Middle Ages, beginning with the medieval devotion to the saints.

Pilgrimages

The Middle Ages were a time of constant traveling and wandering. Not everyone, of course, left his or her native place, and the majority of medieval Christians never traveled more than a five-mile radius beyond where they were born. But a significant minority of Christians devoted months or even years of their lives to making pilgrimages to holy places—the two most visited of which were Rome, with its famous churches, and the shrine of St. James of Compostela (supposedly the tomb of the apostle James the Greater) in northern Spain. And the Crusades were a pilgrimage too, although undertaken for different motives than the pilgrimages to the shrines of Europe.

By the 14th century there were hundreds of shrines which promised holiness for the pilgrims and wealth for the shrines' owners. When Pope Boniface VIII declared the year 1300 a Jubilee Year—a year of remission from temporal punishment due to sin for those traveling to Rome—nearly two million pilgrims came to Rome, donating so much money that priests at St. Peter's had to use rakes to collect it.

Like the cult of relics (see pp. 79-80), pilgrimages were not an entirely religious phenomenon. Chaucer's *Canterbury Tales* accurately depicts pilgrimages as mixtures of devotion, vacation and entertainment. And, as with relics, they also provided an opportunity for the unscrupulous to make money.

The pilgrimage gave birth to the idea of the travel agent: People would sell their services to show Christians the best route to a given shrine, and would furnish guides and maps leading one to the safest and holiest spots. Such agents, through enthusiastic promotional activities, promised this shrine to be the best site for healing and that one the best for finding a suitable mate.

Pilgrimages represented medieval Christians' attempts to make the faith more tangible; they wanted to touch, see and feel the remnants of holiness—whether relics or the site of a saint's burial. Although often colored by superstition, such devotions helped to keep Christianity incarnational—that is, centered on the real world of the senses in which God had become man. Pilgrimages are still popular today, as illustrated by the many ads in Catholic magazines promoting trips to Lourdes and Fatima.

Marian Devotion

Relics and pilgrimages were but the visible manifestation of the medieval cult of the saints. It was actually the power of holiness and virtue epitomized by the saints' lives which drew people to seek after relics and to travel in pilgrimage to holy shrines.

The greatest of saints was the Virgin Mary. Along with the more formalized Mariology we have already considered, a popular literature and folk piety centered on Mary grew up everywhere. This focused especially on miracles worked in her name. Since it was generally accepted that Mary had been bodily assumed into heaven, no one offered relics of her body; but alleged pieces of her clothing traveled far and wide. The cathedral at Chartres in France, for example, proudly displayed the dress she had worn when giving birth to Jesus.

The *Ave Maria* (Hail Mary) became one of the most popular prayers of the day. The Council of Paris at the end of the 12th century decreed that Christians should learn the *Ave Maria* along with the *Pater Noster* (Our Father) and the *Credo* (Apostles' Creed) as the three essential Christian prayers. To assist the faithful to remember how many *Aves* and *Paters* they had recited, someone (we don't know who) conceived of stringing beads together. The first such *rosary* apparently came from a Cistercian monastery, but the Dominicans popularized this devotion.

PARISH LIFE

Whereas the early Church had been principally urban in character, at the height of the Middle Ages most Christians resided in rural areas and engaged in agrarian occupations. Not until the rise of the European city in the 11th and 12th centuries did Christianity begin to regain an urban identity. This meant that from the seventh until at least the 11th century the parish church rather than the diocesan cathedral was the focal point of Christian life.

From Baptism to Burial

As in the early Church, the medieval Christian's first contact with the Church came at Baptism, which by this time meant infant Baptism. Few people were born into non-Christian homes and thus few people in the Middle Ages experienced Baptism as a sign of their conversion to Christianity, as in the early Church. Every small church had its own baptismal font and, owing to the expense involved in making large fonts, Baptism was performed more and more by sprinkling rather than by immersion.

Because of the increasing size of the rural dioceses, Christians had much less contact with their bishops than in earlier days. The parish priest came to represent for them the source and focal point of the sacramental life. Yet in the West (as we saw on p. 70) the bishops still administered the Sacrament of Confirmation themselves. The biographer of Wulfstan, Bishop of Worcester from 1062 to 1095, writes that "in a single day he [Wulfstan] confirmed often as many as two thousand, often three thousand or more, as is established by witnesses of weight."[1]

At the other end of the spectrum from the rite of Christian initiation was the rite of Christian burial, a rite that was repeated much more frequently in the Middle Ages than today. Families were always large—20 childbirths per mother were not abnormal—and infant mortality rates were extremely high, usually close to 50 percent. Thus a good deal of the medieval Christian's parish life was spent at funerals and burials.

Perhaps in no other area of everyday faith did pagan holdovers impinge so strongly on Christian practice than in matters affecting death. It was not at all uncommon for people to be buried with food or with gifts for the pagan deities. The bishops tried to stop such practices with little success, particularly because the parish priests either sympathized with their parishioners or feared to challenge them.

Hell and Purgatory

The popular imagination during the Middle Ages was filled with visions of hell. Anselm the theologian was but one of many writers who has left us a record of the medieval conception of hell: "Sulphurous flames, eddying darkness, swirling with terrible sounds. Worms living in the fire....Devils that burn with us, raging with fire and gnashing your teeth in madness."[2]

In the popular mind the idea of purgatory was not clearly distinct from the idea of heaven until about the mid-12th century. Until that time the everyday faith perceived everyone as either damned or saved; there was no intermediate state. In one recorded vision of the afterlife dated about 1130, a Norman priest recalls seeing his dead friends pass by in review, as it were, exhibiting the tortures they were enduring on account of their sins. One lascivious neighbor rode by seated on a saddle "studded with burning nails."

The most interesting portion of the vision is its observation about the *good* neighbors who trod past the priest's eyes. Even those souls who were bound for "the kingdom of eternal blessedness" were required to have all "unseemliness...burned away in purgatorial fire."[3] In the writer's mind this cleansing fire was not something which burns in a separate place called purgatory; rather, it was a sort of entrance rite for admission to heaven.

Eventually, popular belief in a distinct purgatory caught up with official Church teaching on the subject. As it became more common to have Masses said for a departed soul (a custom made popular by Pope Gregory the Great in the seventh century), it became increasingly necessary for the popular mind to define a place where the soul could stay until its release. This place, of course, was purgatory, which the Second Council of Lyons established as official doctrine in 1274.

Love and Marriage

At the age of 12 in most places boys went to work, either on the manor farm or, if they lived in the city, at the shop of a craftsman to learn a trade. Girls stayed at home practicing the domestic arts and waiting to be found by a suitable mate. Their early years at home fostered literacy, so that girls more often than boys knew how to read, even though females were generally thought incapable of intelligent thought. Men were thought to be suited for manual labor and soldiering, and thus they seldom learned to read, although boys preparing for the priesthood or a profession requiring some degree of literacy were, of course, an exception.

Women were thought to be subservient to men; the Church's canon law specified that wives "should almost be servants." Yet the Church forbade men to practice adultery—an improvement over both Roman and barbarian custom—and protected a woman's right to inherit property. Civil law was harsher than canon law. It permitted wife-beating, although the civil code of one French city permitted this punishment "only in reason." Women were excluded from legislative assemblies and could neither learn a trade nor practice a profession.

Matrimony was only begrudgingly admitted into the rank of the seven sacraments. One Scholastic theologian expressed the prevalent bias against marriage when he wrote, "Marriage, although it is of course a sacrament, does not confer any particular gift of grace, as the other sacraments do, but is a remedy for evil."[4] Popular literature often equaled this scholarly viewpoint, extolling virginity and denigrating marriage. The heroine of nearly every medieval story tries mightily to preserve her virginity and to escape from the clutches of matrimony. Tragically, many a fair damsel was either tricked or forced to submit to marriage and thus "prepare her body for the deed of corruption."[5]

Since there were so many large families in the Middle Ages, the ideal of virginity obviously never actualized itself among the masses; "deeds of corruption" were evidently common among Christian couples. This negative attitude toward sex and marriage—which if anything was even worse in the Byzantine Church—stemmed principally from the ambivalent feelings about women harbored by celibate male clerics. It was a holdover from the Platonic dualism which had infected Christian thought in the early Church.

In the later Middle Ages, as a purely secular literature began to develop, a less jaundiced attitude about marital love gradually began to assert itself in popular religion. The German poet Wolfram von Eschenbach (d. 1220) in his poem *Parzival* described how his hero "discovered the old and new custom of love, and found it pleasant."[6]

From the 13th century on, the popular idea of marriage as something positive increasingly came into conflict with the negative perspective of celibate theologians.

The Mass

It is interesting to find that precisely at the time when Scholastic theology had moved the Eucharist to the center of the sacramental system, the laity participated less and less in the Mass and practically ceased receiving Holy Communion altogether. One account of a typical medieval Mass illustrates graphically how different the laity's role in the liturgy was from the priest's. The priest was separated from the laity by, and celebrated Mass behind, a screen. At the elevation of the host the laity shouted out, "Higher! Higher!" — hoping to get a glimpse of the sacred host which none of them went forward to consume.

Thus, even though attendance at Sunday Mass was obligatory everywhere, reception of the host became increasingly reserved for the priest. In 1215 the Fourth Lateran Council, in an attempt to correct what it saw as an imbalance, decreed that the laity should receive Communion at least once a year. The same council also mandated confession of sins to a priest at least once a year, perhaps as an effort to limit the common practice of confessing one's sins to fellow laypersons (see p. 81).

Since the Mass was celebrated throughout Europe in Latin, few layfolk had any idea of what was going on and, judging from the visitation records of bishops, many of the local priests were not much better off. (Popular demand for Mass celebrated in the vernacular later became increasingly vociferous.)

The Parish Priest

One bishop, upon concluding his diocesan visitation, wrote that the best he could say of his priests was that one of them could read. The ignorance of the clergy in understanding Latin was compounded by the fact that few of them could preach adequately. Even though bishops constantly sought to upgrade their priests' homiletic skills — by producing textbooks on preaching, for example — there is great doubt that the laity gained much real instruction in the faith from the pulpit. With the rise of the mendicants many medieval Christians heard adequate preaching for the first time.

Not all parish priests were dullards, however. Here and there the records reveal striking examples of sanctity and learning. The parish priest Lambert of Liege in the mid-12th century, for example, translated the Acts of the Apostles into the vernacular for his parishioners. He disapproved of the fees commonly charged for administering Baptism and for burials, and he chastised his brother priests who accepted such fees.

At the other end of the spectrum is the scandalous story of the priest who administered a parish in the French village of Montaillou. He was evidently a full-fledged Albigensian, had many mistresses and led his parishioners into lives of drunkenness and debauchery.

The Bible

Every medieval Christian, no matter how humble his or her status in society, knew the Bible and reflected on its meaning. The printed Bible was of course available only in Latin and thus the laity could not read it for themselves. The first vernacular translations were suspect; they usually emanated from heretical sects and were of dubious accuracy in translating the Latin. As a result, the hierarchy tried to limit the laity's contact with the Bible to the preached Bible, or to its visual representation in sacred art.

Pope Gregory the Great (d. 604) had referred to Church paintings as the uneducated person's Bible, and his words served to motivate Christian artists throughout the Middle Ages to paint the scenes of Scripture on the walls, ceilings and windows of every church in Christian Europe. Beginning in the late 11th century another popular means of depicting the Bible began to develop—the tapestry.

Tapestries were long rolls of woven cloth, sometimes more than a hundred feet long, into which were sewn scenes from the Bible. Hung along the walls of churches or in town halls or other public buildings, such as the guild halls of craftsmen, these tapestries kept images from the Bible constantly displayed before the eyes of medieval Christians. Just as today we cannot venture more than a mile without seeing billboards selling beverages, deodorant and toothpaste, so people in the Middle Ages could not enter a public building without being called by artists to reflect on the lessons of Scripture.

Morality

Morality in the Middle Ages was crude. Official misconduct such as bribery, forgery and perjury were as prevalent then as now. A 13th-century preacher condemned all tradesmen as tricksters and cheats. Roads and highways attracted thieves and brigands, and towns were not safe places after dark. In this respect at least, the Middle Ages were thoroughly modern.

To impose law and order on scoundrels the medieval constable was encouraged to be as cruel as possible. Petty criminals were treated leniently by having their faces scarred with a hot poker, fingers chopped off or skin ripped from portions of their body. For serious offenders, typical punishments were boiling in oil, burning at the stake, ripping torsos in half by wild animals and hanging heavy weights to various parts of the body while starvation mercifully dispatched one to the afterlife.

Medieval Christians were medieval before they were Christians. Joan of Arc's English captors cursed continually — so much so that Joan thought "Goddamn" was a common English name. The people of the faith were brutal, lustful, vicious and gluttonous, as well as reverent, humble, awestruck by the gospel and in love with Jesus, Mary and the saints.

Neither before nor since has there been an age of such contradiction. Francis of Assisi spoke of his epoch as "times of malice and iniquity." And a Franciscan scientist named Roger Bacon (1214-1292) believed that the world had never witnessed so much ignorance, sin, corruption and lechery. He marveled that in the face of such wickedness so many people still professed belief in the gospel.

Perhaps we could best compare the Middle Ages to our own day by saying that medieval Christians had not yet devised the technology to conceal their sins and so committed them blatantly. We moderns, on the other hand, can consider ourselves moral only because we have managed to hide the evils we practice: concentration camps, aerial bombardment, racial discrimination, the impoverishment of Third-World countries, legalized abortion. The victims of our cruelty rarely confront us as persons; people in the Middle Ages were at least forthright about their barbarism.

Churches

Situated in the midst of this boiling caldron of vulgarity was a powerful countervailing symbol, the local church. The typical rural church was little more than a crude box; attached to it was a shed where the parish priest lived. Yet even this inelegant edifice represented for the medieval Christians the gateway to eternal life. As the faithful entered, the crude realities of life were left behind. Once within they encountered the power of a living faith — sketched however rudely on the walls or windows, preached however humbly by the pastor and delivered into one's very soul by the Eucharist.

In the local church medieval Christians played out their quest for wholeness. Here heaven and earth were united in the liturgy of the Church and its sacraments; here one communed with the eternal family — Jesus, Mary and the saints; here one sought forgiveness of sins and restoration to holiness (wholeness of relationship with God).

Since the church came to be the focal point of the Christian's quest for wholeness, medieval church architecture constantly sought better ways to express that wholeness. The most magnificent expressions of this evolving architecture were the Gothic cathedrals of the 12th and 13th centuries: Notre Dame, Reims, Amiens, Chartres, Canterbury, Winchester, Strasbourg—the list goes on and on.

Gothic architecture evolved from Romanesque churches, which had been somber, sturdy, bulky structures that, in effect, announced to the viewer "Security, stability, order." By the 12th century, however, with the development of contemplative spirituality and Scholastic philosophy, medieval Christians had turned from the mundane pursuit of security alone to the pursuit of spiritual wholeness and abstract speculation.

Just as Scholastic theologians were breaking new ground and no longer revering tradition for tradition's sake, so too church architects—we know almost none of their names—began to experiment with new styles. As if to mimic the lofty, abstract thought of an Anselm, or to follow Bernard of Clairvaux to the height of mystical union, Gothic architects constructed their churches on pointed ribbed vaults, reaching to dizzying heights never believed possible before.

Like the developing stages of a Scholastic's theological argument—point building on point until the conclusion follows by necessity—so too each level of a Gothic cathedral built on the one that preceded it, bringing the whole to fulfillment in a dazzling conclusion of light, color and grace, crowned by a stained-glass mandala which presented in one circle, as it were, the faith in its entirety.

Not the slightest detail of these great structures lacked a purpose; everything was calculated to draw the viewer into a sense of wholeness and completion. Once inside one of these living organisms, the entire panoply of the faith unfolded before the believer. Processions, liturgies, Gregorian chant, incense, the art in the windows, the tapestries on the walls—all conspired to deliver one from the state of disintegration and chaos which characterized the outside world into a state of harmony with God. Despite their many faults the people of the faith knew how to worship. The medieval cathedral was the most magnificent expression of humanity's quest for wholeness ever constructed.

The Secularization of Culture

In the life of the cathedral one found drama, music, art, sculpture and architecture all in one place. Consequently, in the high Middle

Ages culture and faith were one. The Catholic Church completely dominated the individual's intellectual and moral development through liturgy, sacraments and devotion; it successfully established an integrated pattern for human knowledge, belief and behavior that fulfilled the medieval Christian's quest for wholeness.

Beginning about the 12th century, however, this Catholic culture began to leave the confines of the parish church and the cathedral. With the development of a money economy, literacy, cities and universities, a new type of Catholic culture began to circulate throughout Western society — a culture influenced by lay people rather than by the clergy.

New Literary Forms

Medieval writers began to develop a new genre, the *geste* ("deeds"), a quasi-historical chronicle depicting the derring-do of national heroes. The *Gesta Francorum* ("Deeds of the Franks"), for example, was a Norman knight's account of the First Crusade. The *Gesta Romanorum* ("Deeds of the French") was a collection of short tales, each with a moral, widely read by laypersons in England and France.

Along with the *geste*, the 12th century witnessed the development of historical writing, such as the *Major Chronicle* of Matthew Paris (1200-1259) and the *History of St. Louis* by Jean Sire de Joinville. These Latin works were matched by epics and sagas written in the newly developing national languages — *Beowulf* in English, the *Song of Roland* in French, the *Song of the Nibelungs* in German and *Poem of the Cid* in Spanish.

The 12th century also gave birth to medieval poetry. Bishop Peter Damian (1007-1072), in addition to many reform writings, found time to write poetry rivaling anything produced by classical Latin poets.

It was through poetry more than any other medium that religious culture gradually became secularized. In 1227 the Church felt it necessary to condemn the rhymes composed by poets known as "Goliardi," named after Golias — a fictional character of one of the poets. The Goliards — made up of both laymen and priests — wandered from place to place reciting verses which satirized the foolishness and misconduct of prelates and nobles. Goliardic poetry, in addition to being a subtle form of protest, gradually embraced themes that were frankly secular, in particular the exaltation of a life devoted to wine, women and song.

Eleanor of Aquitaine: Patron of Romantic Love

The new poetry was a natural outgrowth of a culture gradually becoming feminized. Romanesque architecture—massive and fortress-like—had epitomized the Middle Ages' *animus*, or male personality traits. Gothic architecture, on the other hand—with its beauty, lightness and grace—brought into tangible form the *anima*, or female traits. In the same way the new literature—above all the new poetry—ennobled and dignified women.

The summit of the new feminine culture was reached in the court of one of the Middle Ages' most remarkable women, Eleanor of Aquitaine (d. 1204), wife first of a French and then of an English king, and mother of two other kings, John of England and his brother, Richard the Lionhearted.

Aquitaine, in the southwest of France, was an important duchy coveted by kings of both France and England; Eleanor had inherited it from her grandfather. She turned her court at Toulouse into a haven for wandering poets and patronized the newly developing secular culture. Motivated by the increasing devotion to Mary and the softening of spirituality produced by the Cistercian emphasis on contemplation, Eleanor's court poets proclaimed the beauty and dignity of women. By the mid-12th century these poets had come to be known as *troubadours*.

The troubadours proclaimed romantic love as the greatest virtue, an expression in physical form of the union between God and the soul which was effected by contemplative prayer. Although frankly sensual—a fact which disturbed many churchmen—the troubadours' poetry was nonetheless delicate and graceful in its proclamation of man's love for woman. The German equivalent of the troubadours were the *minnesingers* ("love singers"). They, too, elevated woman to a status never before dreamt of in this warlike age.

The *Chanson de Geste*

As the poets brought civility and gentleness to feudal courts, male warlords themselves were given a new genre of literature, one which justified warfare by submitting it to feminine virtue. This genre was the *chanson de geste* ("song of deeds"), epic poems depicting the hero going bravely off to battle in order to protect his beloved at home, and either dying with her name on his lips or returning to give her some token of his victory. (It does not require much imagination to recognize this chivalrous ideal in modern popular culture, especially in the American sagas of the old West, where cowboy actors like Gary Cooper were but medieval knights in different dress.)

The most popular of the *chansons* were the tales of King Arthur and his knights of the Round Table—Gawain, Percival, Lancelot—all of whom fought bravely to defend the honor of Queen Guinevere,

Arthur's wife, who of course none of the knights could ever marry.

Yet this did not matter. The medieval poets separated romantic love from sex and marriage. The latter were physical necessities engaged in for economic reasons and for the procreation of the species. Romantic love, on the other had, was a purely spiritual phenomenon; through it medieval man could glorify his ideal woman, putting her on the same pedestal as Mary and the saints.

To us the role of the male in the *chansons* may appear to be little more than a childish projection of selfish fantasies onto women. For medieval man, however, the *chansons* were a powerful channel—along with Marian devotion and contemplative spirituality—for the expression of his inner *anima*. In the person of his idealized beloved, the medieval male found personal wholeness as he shed momentarily his cloak of cruelty and belligerence.

A Dream Unravels

The actual situation, however, never matched the ideal. While the ideal woman—the pure virgin of faultless character and entrancing beauty fantasized in the troubadours' poetry—was worshiped and protected, one's actual wife or daughter was usually treated as a servant rather than as a queen. The Middle Ages were pockmarked with contradiction, even as our own times are.

We find this contradiction well illustrated in the most famous of medieval poems, *Roman de la Rose* (the word *roman* meant any poem written in French, the *romance* language). The *Roman de la Rose* was an allegory of 22,000 lines written in two sections by two different authors 40 years apart. The first section, dating to about 1225, tells the story of a young man who dreams of a beautiful garden in which grows a splendid rose (symbolizing his beloved), surrounded by thorns (symbolizing the perils and pitfalls associated with the pursuit of his lover). This section of the poem is a typical troubadour love ballad glorifying woman and romantic love.

The second section, however, is written after 1260—in a generation which had soured on the Crusades and grown skeptical over the debates of argumentative Scholastics. Here the author changes the character of woman altogether. Now woman is contemptuous, seductive and deceitful. She is no longer an idealized virgin, but an object of sexual gratification. The parallels with our own day's view of woman are obvious. By the mid-13th century the quest for wholeness, so masterfully summarized in the love poetry of the previous generation's *chansons*, had become jaded by the realities of warfare and social unrest.

The medieval quest for wholeness reached its peak in these high

Middle Ages, epitomized by such persons as Bernard of Clairvaux, Innocent III, Thomas Aquinas and Eleanor of Aquitaine. Henceforth the quest for wholeness becomes an unattainable goal, a Holy Grail which only the purest of Galahads can dream of finding. For one bright shining moment the Middle Ages had held the Grail in its hands. Now, as the medieval syntheses of faith and reason, Church and State, spirit and flesh, *animus* and *anima* begin to unravel, we track not the quest for wholeness but the path of disintegration.

CHAPTER TEN

THE POPES RESIST REFORM

**From the Babylonian Captivity
to the Renaissance Papacy (1305-1447)**

In this chapter we pick up where we left off in Chapter Seven (with the Babylonian Captivity in 1305) and trace the external development of the Church to the beginning of the Renaissance papacy in 1447. From the pontificate of Pope Clement V (1305-1314) to that of Pope Eugene IV (1431-1447), the hierarchical Church would struggle in vain to reimpose on Christian Europe the concept of papal supremacy which had reached its zenith under Pope Innocent III. The popes of the late Middle Ages (1300-1450), however, would increasingly succumb to new forces dominating Christian society. These forces would prevent forever the reestablishment of a supranational Christendom under the authority of the pope.

Let's see what these new forces were, and how they affected the papacy's continued quest to impose external unity and wholeness on Christian society.

THE AVIGNON PAPACY

We will begin by surveying the period from 1305 to 1378, when seven popes reigned from their Babylonian Captivity in the French city of Avignon.

Clement V

Pope Clement V (1305-1314) was a Frenchman, the former archbishop of Bordeaux in southwest France. Clement was a docile servant of the French king, Philip IV (the Fair), who ordered Clement to invalidate the onerous bulls (see p. 101) issued by Pope Boniface VIII. Clement packed the College of Cardinals with his nephews* and French allies, thereby transforming the College from an Italian into a French body.

John XXII

Clement V's acquiescence to the French king's every wish left the Church a shameful legacy. When he died, 18 French and seven Italian cardinals could not reach a decision as to Clement's successor for two years. Finally, King Louis X locked up the cardinals in a Dominican monastery and ordered them to select one of four candidates from a list he had drawn up himself. John XXII (1316-1334) was the cardinals' choice.

John is noteworthy for little more than his constant political scheming, and for propagating the heretical doctrine that the souls of the elect do not experience the beatific vision until after the general judgment at the end of the world. Umberto Eco in *The Name of the Rose* gives us a good portrait of John's devious and selfish character.

Benedict XII

The cardinals meeting in Avignon to elect John's successor tried to assure the future pope's return to Rome by extracting from all candidates a promise to withdraw from Avignon. The former Cistercian, James Fournier, now a cardinal, was chosen as Pope Benedict XII (1334-1342). He immediately reneged on his promise to return to Rome and began the construction of a papal palace in Avignon. Like his predecessors, Benedict was a pliant tool of the French king, supporting the king's demand for the payment of taxes from French churches.

In Germany, bishops and barons harshly criticized the pope's submission to the French crown and declared their disapproval of the French-papal marriage. Two prominent political theorists, William of Ockham and Marsilius of Padua—about whom we shall say more shortly—wrote treatises rejecting the temporal authority of the popes, as well as the idea of papal primacy altogether.

Clement VI

Cardinal Peter Roger from Limousin in central France was

---

*This nepotism would continue to be a common papal vice. Pope Alexander III remarked that since God had deprived bishops of sons the devil had given them nephews.

elected as Pope Clement VI (1342-1352). Clement was pope during the height of the Hundred Years' War (discussed later) between England and France. He finished construction of the palace in Avignon which Benedict XII had begun, and turned the papal court into a luxurious showpiece of wealth and grandeur rivaling anything the kings of Europe could produce. He openly staffed the Curia with friends and relatives and outdid all his predecessors in creating an aura of pomp and majesty, declaring that previous popes had not really understood how a pope was supposed to live.

At the very height of the papacy's worldly pretensions, a plague known as the Black Death (see p. 150) consumed Europe (1347-1352), carrying nearly a third of the population to its grave. Many Christians detected in the plague a sign of God's displeasure over the corruption of St. Peter's office.

Innocent VI

Another French cardinal succeeded Clement VI as Pope Innocent VI (1352-1362). Innocent VI seriously considered returning the papacy to Rome. A Roman politician, Cola di Rienzo, had gained control of the Roman lower classes, overthrowing the patricians who ruled Rome and establishing himself as "tribune of the people" in 1347. Cola had entreated Clement VI to return to Rome to no avail. Pope Innocent VI, however, saw Cola as a tool for the destruction of the powerful noble families who had gained control of the Papal States during the popes' absence from Rome.

Thus Pope Innocent named Cola "senator" in 1353. Cola worked enthusiastically with the pope's legate in Italy to reconsolidate the pope's power over the Papal States. Cola and Innocent shared the dream of revitalizing the ancient Roman imperial grandeur under the spiritual headship of the pope and the secular leadership of a popularly elected tribune such as Cola. Their dream was shattered when Roman nobles allied long enough to overthrow Cola and kill him.

Urban V

When Innocent VI died, he was succeeded by a Benedictine abbot from a noble French family, who took the name Urban V (1362-1370). Urban was the only Avignon pope who had a spiritual temperament. He disgusted the hangers-on at court by continuing to wear his monk's garb and by trying to impose monastic discipline on the Curia—an impossible task which led Urban to dismiss a good portion of the Curia.

Urban was a scandal to the many French cardinals who had never dreamed that a Frenchman would try to do away with the monarchical elegance of the papal court. Urban earnestly wanted to return the papacy to Rome but met stiff resistance from the largely French College of Cardinals. With his own military escort, however, Urban set out for Rome in 1367. He stayed long enough to restore several badly disheveled Roman churches but, finding too many noble families opposed to a French pope, went back to Avignon and died.

Gregory XI

Under Pope Gregory XI (1370-1378) the papacy finally did return to Rome. The growing insecurity of the French political situation, caused by the prolongation of the Hundred Years' War, led Gregory to conclude that France was no longer a safe haven for the popes.

Wisely the pope first sent his army to Italy to subdue the Roman nobility before he himself crossed the Alps. In spite of the general state of anarchy caused by warfare between city-states such as Florence and Milan, Gregory entered Rome on January 17, 1377.

The papacy's Babylonian Captivity had ended. But the popes' 73-year stay in France had reduced the authority and influence of the papacy to its lowest point in centuries.

SPIRITUAL VS. SECULAR AUTHORITY: NEW CONCEPTIONS

While the popes reigned as resplendent monarchs at Avignon, attending to their personal concerns and ambitions, the Church languished for lack of leadership and guidance. If the popes were ignorant of or simply disinterested in this sad state of affairs, many others were not. The Avignon papacy motivated Christian thinkers to reappraise papal primacy, Church authority in general, and the relationship between Church and State. Thus, while the popes idled away their hours in intrigue at Avignon, others were busy formulating a new conception of spiritual and secular authority.

William of Ockham

Born in England in 1285, William of Ockham entered the Franciscans and studied and taught at Oxford. In 1323 he was accused of several errors and was summoned to Avignon by Pope John XXII. While his works were being examined at Avignon he continued to write theology and philosophy.

In 1327 the minister-general of the Franciscans asked Ockham to study the Franciscan dispute over poverty (see pp. 98-99). When

Ockham responded by writing that Pope John was heretical in teaching that Christ and the apostles had not lived in poverty, Ockham was forced to flee Avignon. He went to the court of King Louis of Bavaria, who granted him refuge. From about 1331 on, when Ockham was expelled from the Franciscans at the pope's insistence, he turned more and more in his writings to an attack on papal primacy.

Nominalism and Skepticism

Ockham was a Nominalist (see p. 135). For him, every permanent substance is uniquely individual. Even God has no universal attributes, for if God were possessed of attributes such as intellect or will, Ockham said, these attributes themselves must of necessity be divine, and thus God would not be one being but several. The Trinity, he said, is logically impossible and must be blindly accepted on faith. Through this approach Ockham drove a wedge between faith and reason, destroying the synthesis between the two which Aquinas had constructed.

As Ockham's philosophy gained hold in the universities, they become centers of skepticism. Absolutes such as human nature, truth or goodness were subjected to logical attack. Scholars began to question the means of knowing and thus the validity of knowledge itself. They wondered if anything in the mind could not simply be a false abstraction from an individual.

Nothing was certain and thus everything became possible. It is this climate of nominalistic skepticism which leads the narrator of Eco's *The Name of the Rose* to conclude his tale on the pessimistic note: *"Stat rosa pristina nomine, nomina nuda tenemus,"* which I translate as, "The rose of yesteryear is but a name, mere names are left to us."

There can be little doubt that the events of the times greatly influenced this new way of thinking. A devastating war between England and France lasting over a century, a plague that wiped out huge numbers of people and, finally, the successors of Peter "the rock" conducting themselves like royal princes who cared not a whit for the Church's spiritual well-being—all caused people to wonder if there were anything certain in life after all.

Ockham's Theory of Church and State

Because of his Nominalist orientation, Ockham believed that the Church as a "universal," as the Body of Christ representing all individual Christians, did not exist in and of itself. The Church, Ockham said, is merely a community comprised of the sum of its members.

Further, Ockham said, the Church cannot be identified with the clergy. The entire Church as the community of all the faithful is superior to any of its members, including priests, bishops and pope. Finally, Ockham taught, the pope's authority is limited purely to what is essential for the salvation of souls. "All else," Ockham wrote, "even though it be spiritual, he must not command, lest the law of the Gospel become a law of slavery."[1] The Church may delegate to a council comprised of its elected representatives the power to act on behalf of all, but it is only such a council which has the primacy of authority in the Church, not pope or clergy.

Marsilius of Padua

Marsilius of Padua, an Italian layman and scholar, went beyond Ockham in granting autonomy to the individual. Marsilius's principal work was *Defender of the Peace* (1324). In it he describes the State as the unifying force of society, completely superior to the Church. The State derives its authority from the people, who may intervene at any time to remove a ruler.

For Marsilius, the Church has no inherent authority whatsoever; whatever authority it has is given to it by the State, which may withdraw its grant of authority at will. The Church may not own property but may use property loaned to it by the State. The pope and the bishops are not divinely authorized to rule the Church; their offices are of purely human institution.

The so-called Petrine primacy, Marsilius said, is derived solely from the *Donation of Constantine*, a document in which Emperor Constantine the Great had supposedly granted Pope Sylvester I (314-335) primacy over the other major sees of Christendom. (After Marsilius's time the *Donation* was proved to be a forgery. Marsilius, however, believed it to be authentic.) Since this primacy was created by civil authority through the *Donation*, Marsilius said, it could likewise be terminated by the same authority and, by implication, had already been so terminated.

The true primacy in the Church, Marsilius said, lies not in bishops or popes but in general councils composed of laymen as well as clergy. Thus, for Marsilius the Church was not a hierarchical institution but "the totality of the faithful who believe in Christ's name and invoke him."[2] Marsilius went even beyond Ockham, who was willing to admit that Christ had conferred some real authority on Peter and his successors. Ockham recognized two powers, pope and emperor, exercising their respective powers in two different realms. Marsilius of Padua, however, recognized only one power authorized to govern human affairs—the State—and, ultimately, the people.

136

THE WESTERN SCHISM

As if to fuel the flames ignited by the writings of Ockham and Marsilius (both of whose writings were condemned), the College of Cardinals in 1378 blundered the Church into schism by electing two different popes, Urban VI and Clement VII, following the death of Pope Gregory XI.

This schism resulted from the fact that several French cardinals had refused to leave Avignon when Gregory XI returned to Rome (see p. 134). Therefore all the cardinals were not present in Rome when rioting citizens invaded the conclave, even while Gregory's body was being buried, and demanded the election of a Roman pope.

Acting under the duress of the moment, the cardinals hastily elected Urban VI. As soon as order was restored, however, some cardinals expressed their opposition to Urban and sought a new election. Those French cardinals still residing in Avignon won over some of the disgruntled Italian cardinals and secured the election of the cardinal-bishop of Geneva, who became Pope Clement VII. Urban VI had to hire mercenaries to keep himself on the papal throne in Rome, while Clement VII stayed in Avignon.

Each pope sought to win kings, princes, universities, bishops and even saints over to his side (see map, p. 138). No one knew who was rightfully pope. This situation caused drastic confusion throughout the Church, as illustrated by the prayer authorized in the canon of the Mass by the bishop of Toledo for "whoever is the true pope."

Urban VI did everyone a favor in 1389 by dying. But the Italian conclave of cardinals, instead of doing the sensible thing by simply accepting Clement VII, held another election, choosing Boniface IX as pope. Not to be outdone, the French cardinals—upon the death of Clement VII—likewise refused to act sensibly and elected another Avignon pope, Benedict XIII. After Boniface, two more Italians were elected to the papacy, so that by 1406 the situation could be summarized as follows:

The Roman Line*	The Avignon Line
Urban VI (1378-1389)	Clement VII (1378-1394)
Boniface IX (1389-1404)	
Innocent VII (1404-1406)	Benedict XIII (1394-1423)
Gregory XII (1406-1415)	

*The Catholic Church today recognizes the Roman line as authentic popes and rejects the Avignon line as anti-popes.

EUROPE AT THE TIME OF THE PAPAL SCHISM (1378-1417)

Moslem Area

Officially Loyal to Rome but Shifting Local Allegiances

Loyal to the Pope in Rome

Loyal to the Pope in Avignon

The Council of Pisa

By 1409 both factions of cardinals had acknowledged that the schism could not continue indefinitely, and they agreed to meet in council at Pisa to settle the controversy. Five hundred delegates attended: 24 cardinals, 80 archbishops, 80 abbots and a substantial number of lesser clergy, as well as lay noblemen. They deposed both Gregory XII and Benedict XIII and elected the cardinal of Milan as Pope Alexander V (rejected today as an anti-pope). Since neither Gregory XII nor Benedict XIII accepted the council's decision, however, there were now three popes instead of two.

Although the Council of Pisa failed to settle the schism, and in fact made it worse, the council was of great significance for the future. Stimulated by the writings of Ockham and Marsilius, the delegates to the council engaged in heady discussions concerning Church authority. Many council delegates began to take seriously the idea that the pope was not the head of the Church. In doing so the delegates saw themselves as standing in the best tradition of the early Church, when councils and not popes had decided questions of dogma, jurisdiction and authority. (Also, this was the first Council since the Council of Jerusalem—Acts 15—which allowed laymen to vote.)

Some delegates felt that the Church needed to be redefined according to the theories of Ockham and Marsilius. Eventually, however, the majority remained faithful to the concept of papal primacy by electing another pope. But even this majority came away from Pisa convinced of the need for regularly recurring councils which would govern the Church along with the pope.

The Council of Pisa gave birth to a more widely accepted conciliar conception of the Church. As new crises threatened the unity of the Church, the conciliar thinking at Pisa solidified into a broadly based movement.

THE CALL FOR CHURCH REFORM

It should come as no surprise to learn that papal schism and corruption inspired many Christians to seek a drastic, overall reform of the Church. In the continuing quest for wholeness, reformers demanded that the Church be whole in its authority and holy in its conduct.

John Wycliffe

A philosopher and theologian at Oxford, John Wycliffe (1330-1384) mistrusted the new skepticism injected into academic life by Ockham and his followers. His philosophy, like that of the earliest

Scholastics, was profoundly religious in character.

Wycliffe depended on the Bible and the Fathers rather than on logical speculation for his philosophical premises. The more he pursued Scripture, the more he became convinced of an essential distinction between the Church as an institution with a visible hierarchy and the Church as a purely spiritual entity. The latter, he believed, was the true Church, and if the institutional Church had any authority or jurisdiction at all it was derived from the spiritual Church.

In *On Civil Dominion* (1375) Wycliffe wrote that all clerical authority depended on grace, and that if a clergyman was found not to be living in grace he could be stripped of his ministerial authority by the secular ruler. In other writings he upheld the Bible (which he insisted should be translated into the vernacular) as the "sole exemplar" of orthodox Christianity and the final arbiter of doctrine, arguing that the papacy was a non-scriptural office. (This teaching was but a further development of the movement discussed on pp. 97-98.)

In *On Apostasy* (1382) Wycliffe condemned clerical orders as a whole, and called on the king to abolish the English Church and to establish a radically new body based on the original Christian community described in the New Testament. He condemned transubstantiation, purgatory, confession of sins to priests, the cult of relics and saints, indulgences, monasticism and the entire sacramental system.

The Social Revolt

Wycliffe wrote in a time of profound social unrest. The breakdown of feudalism, the impoverishment of many knights and landed gentry, the turmoil of the Hundred Years' War and bubonic plague—all brought the entire structure of society to near anarchy. In Wycliffe's England the peasantry had been bled white by their kings' taxes, which then were poured into the bottomless pit of the Hundred Years' War.

A poll tax levied in 1380 was the straw that broke the camel's back. Peasants and urban industrial workers (principally in the wool mills) erupted in revolt. King Richard II saw his government teeter toward collapse. Eventually, however, the king prevailed. Rebel ringleaders were drawn and quartered; the rest were beaten by the king's soldiers and ordered back to their subservient tasks. They obeyed but harbored bitter resentment toward all authority, whether civil or ecclesiastical.

The peasants' movement had become associated in the minds of the upper classes with Wycliffe, even though he had had nothing to do with the revolt. Wycliffe's followers had at first been limited to a small group of like-minded scholars at Oxford, but his views increasingly became a sort of rallying point for the popular dissatisfaction over royal taxation and clerical wealth. Wycliffe thus became a symbol of protest for the poorer classes.

Thus, the peasants' revolt served as a catalyst for the suppression of Wycliffe's doctrines, and he was forced to resign from his teaching position. After his death in 1384 his supporters became known as Lollards ("chanters"), a name which eventually applied to anyone in England who advocated Church reform. The Council of Constance in 1415 (see below) formally condemned Wycliffe's doctrines.

John Hus

There would appear to be no more unlikely supporters for Wycliffe's ideas than the subjects of the far-off kingdom of Bohemia (present-day Czechoslovakia). But, because the Hapsburg prince Albert I had acquired the crown of Bohemia in 1306, Bohemia gradually came to play an increasingly important role in European politics, eventually becoming the center of the Western empire.

Just like England, Bohemia had a large and restless peasantry dissatisfied with the Church's and the aristocracy's control of the land. And, as in England, the Bohemian peasantry identified the Church as the partner of the aristocracy and thus as a source of oppression.

King Wenceslaus of Bohemia had married his sister to King Richard II of England in 1382, so there was a good deal of cultural and intellectual exchange between the two kingdoms. One of those who profited from this exchange was a Bohemian peasant priest named John Hus (1372-1415).

Hus became Dean of Philosophy at the University of Prague in 1401 and openly advocated many of Wycliffe's teachings. He initially received the support of the Bohemian clergy, including that of the archbishop of Prague. But as his attacks on the clergy became more and more inflammatory, the archbishop forbade Hus from further preaching.

King Wenceslaus, by placing the University of Prague under Hus's sole leadership, made Hus a champion both of Wycliffe's doctrine and of Bohemian independence from Rome. Hus was now a dangerous symbol, and in 1411 Pope Gregory XII excommunicated him. Hus left Prague and found refuge among various Bohemian nobles. In 1413 he wrote *On the Church*, virtually a summary of Wycliffe's teachings and a work which became immensely popular in Bohemia.

THE COUNCIL OF CONSTANCE AND
CONCILIAR REFORM

When King Sigismund of Bohemia succeeded King Wenceslaus, he called for a council to meet at Constance in 1414 (in southern Germany not far from Zurich). His purpose was to end the papal schism, reform the Church and eradicate heresy.

Heresy Condemned

Hus appealed his excommunication by the pope directly to the council. Sigismund gave Hus his personal pledge of safe conduct to and from the council. Suitably protected — or so Hus thought — he traveled to Constance in November.

The council condemned Wycliffe's teachings in their entirety and ordered that his body be exhumed from consecrated ground and reburied elsewhere. John Hus received the chance to express his views at a public hearing, which led to an indictment of heresy against him. When he refused to recant he was burned at the stake, King Sigismund's guarantee of safe conduct going up in flames with him.

Papal Schism Ended

The teachings of Hus and Wycliffe were not the only items on the agenda at the Council of Constance (1414-1418). There were still three popes: the intractable rivals Benedict XIII and Gregory XII, and the successor of Pope Alexander V (who had died in 1410) — Pope John XXIII (regarded today as an anti-pope). It was John XXIII who opened and presided over the council. As at Pisa, there was a strong lay delegation in attendance — especially German counts, princes and university teachers. Notably, a delegation from the Byzantine Church was also present, making Constance the most ecumenical Christian assembly of the Middle Ages.

The council conducted its affairs in 45 sessions over a period of three and a half years. The sentiment of the council was to depose John XXIII along with the other two popes in favor of an entirely new pontiff. John's detractors circulated accusations of immorality against him and charged him with having murdered his predecessor, Alexander V. John did not help his cause by fleeing from Constance in disguise and under cover of darkness on March 20, 1415.

The delegates then enacted a decree declaring:

> This council holds its power directly from Christ; everyone, no matter his rank or office, even if it be papal, is bound to obey it in whatever

pertains to faith, to the extirpation of the schism, as well as to the reform of the church in its head and in its members.[3]

For the moment, conciliar primacy replaced papal primacy as the basis of Church authority.

John XXIII was forcibly returned to Constance, condemned for his immorality and deposed on May 29, 1415. To help matters along, Pope Gregory XII finally abdicated on July 4, 1415. Yet, Benedict XIII stubbornly held his ground. Two years later, after numerous attempts to persuade Benedict to abdicate, he was "re-deposed" (see p. 139) on July 16, 1417.

The council then changed the election procedure for the successor pope, decreeing that the cardinals plus six representatives each (who could be laymen) from five different nations would conduct the papal election. Meeting in conclave, this electoral assembly chose the cardinal-deacon Oddo Colonna of Rome who, after being ordained a priest and consecrated a bishop, was installed as Pope Martin V (1417-1431). Benedict XIII continued to lose support until his death in 1423, and thus the election of Martin V effectively ended the schism.

Besides ending the papal schism, the council also issued decrees on reform and on the teachings of Wycliffe and Hus.

Conciliarism: Hope for Reform

The council tried to perpetuate itself and its reforming impulses by ruling that only a regularly recurring general council could permanently reform the Church. The delegates succinctly set forth their attitudes on conciliar reform in a typical manifesto circulating at the council:

> The pope has no absolute and full authority; he is not allowed to call himself "supreme priest" but only "first among bishops." His reserving all business of his subjects to himself, his conferring of dignities and benefices, is a recent invention of the Latin Church. All this power in the hands of a single man! Only Christ and the universal Church in a general council are permitted to have such power.[4]

Before they elected Martin V, the delegates had decreed that a general council was to be convened at intervals of five, seven and then every 10 years. The council took as its motto "Without a council, no reform" and extracted from the pope-to-be a pledge to convene regularly recurring councils.

Thus, by electing Martin V the council delegates *thought* they were electing a new type of pope—one who supported the conciliar ideal and who would divest himself of monarchical prerogatives. The delegates were to discover shortly after Martin's coronation, however, that the new pope had no intention of keeping his word to convene a new council. In fact, Martin became an implacable foe of conciliarism and an ardent advocate of the medieval monarchical papacy which the Council of Constance had intended to terminate.

Foes of Conciliarism: Martin V and Eugene IV

Martin's first significant act on becoming pope was to dissolve the Council of Constance. Two delegations of cardinals then presented Martin with proposals for the reform council which was supposed to convene five years after Constance. Although Martin rejected the cardinals' proposals, in 1431 he capitulated to the cardinals' ever more urgent demand for a council and convened the Council of Basle in Switzerland. Martin died before the council could accomplish anything.

Martin's successor, Pope Eugene IV, tried to dissolve the Council of Basle in a bull issued on December 18, 1431, but the delegates ignored the pope. At this point the council consisted of only 14 bishops and abbots and a small number of lesser clergy. But, though the delegates were small in number, they had the enthusiastic support of many nobles and of various universities.

The delegates called for each newly elected pope to swear to uphold the conciliar reform principle and to declare the council's supremacy over the Curia. In a clever attempt to divert attention from the council's reform efforts, Eugene invited the Byzantines to the West for negotiations on reunion. Since the Byzantines would travel no farther than Italy, Eugene declared the Council of Basle disbanded "for the sake of unity" and reconvened it first at Ferrara and then at Florence.

Ecumenical Subterfuge: The Council of Florence

The council which Eugene had convened at Florence (1438-1443) attended not to the matter of reforming the Western Church but to reuniting the Western and Eastern Churches. The Byzantine Emperor John VIII and Patriarch Joseph of Constantinople led an impressive delegation of Byzantine theologians to Florence, where Latins and Greeks began their discussions over the long-standing theological issues separating the two Churches.

Along with relatively minor matters, such as the use of unleavened bread in the Western liturgy and the dispute over purgatory, the two sides also tackled the central controversies—the *filioque* question and the question of papal authority. When arguments from both sides availed nothing, the Greek delegation eventually proposed a solution which amounted to saying that, while neither side erred in its doctrine, each expressed its doctrines differently.

Both sides signed a decree of union—a decree worded so ambiguously and evasively as to be theologically inconclusive on any of the major issues. The decree ended with the innocuous statement, "Between the Western and Eastern Fathers there can be no contradiction since they are all illuminated by the Holy Spirit."

When the Byzantines returned home, the populace read the decree of union as a capitulation to papal authority and thus condemned it. Several Byzantine bishops who had signed the decree recanted.

Within a decade, however, any question of "union" between East and West was rendered completely moot. In 1453 the Ottoman Sultan Muhammad II ("the Conqueror") entered the besieged capital of Constantinople and captured it. The Byzantine Empire, the last repository of Roman imperial greatness, was utterly destroyed. The city named for the first Christian emperor was no more; in its place was created a new capital—Istanbul—soon to display a new culture and a new religion.

Meanwhile, in the West, the popes felt confident that they had sufficiently deflected the blows of conciliarism and returned the papacy to its monarchical splendor. For a few decades they managed to live on in unbothered opulence. But before long they would discover that in resisting reform, they had brought down upon their heads the Reformation.

CHAPTER ELEVEN

THE WANING OF THE MIDDLE AGES

Late-Medieval Christianity: Behavior, Thought and Faith

In this chapter we will discuss events, theology and spirituality to the end of the Middle Ages. We begin by discussing the Middle Ages' last experiment with warfare.

THE HUNDRED YEARS' WAR: 1337-1453

Ever since William the Conqueror had led his Norman troops across the Channel to England in 1066 (see p. 66), England had claimed ownership of Normandy. Dynastic marriages between French and English monarchs since William's time had brought even more French land under English control. For three centuries various French lords had been bound by oaths of fealty to English kings claiming dominion over French territory.

In addition, as England had become more and more reliant on its wool trade,* it had formed a mercantile alliance with weavers and capitalist investors in Flanders. This relationship was threatened in 1328 when the French King Philip VI annexed Flanders as his vassal state.

Philip had become king in an unusual way. The last Capetian king of France had died in 1328 with no male heir. Since the French refused to allow a *female* descendant of the Capetian line to succeed to the throne (no queen ever ruled as titular sovereign of France), King

---

*The English kings used to sit on wool sacks in Parliament in order to dramatize the nation's dependence on this product.

Edward III of England claimed the French crown as his. (Edward, through a previous dynastic marriage, was the grandson of King Philip IV of France.) The French barons, however, elected a count of Valois (northeast France) as the first monarch in the new Valois dynasty (1328-1515): Philip VI.

In England, King Edward fulminated at the French barons' decision to bypass him, and his advisers persuaded him that France was a ripe plum waiting to be plucked. Piecing together the various components—English claims to French territory in Normandy, France's control of England's best wool outlet, a French king surrounded by ambitious and independent nobles, and the rumor that King Philip was about to leave for the Crusades—Edward decided to strike. In 1337, with chivalrous aplomb, Edward notified Philip that he was about to invade France.

The ensuing Hundred Years' War lasted until 1453, but fighting was not continuous. One can identify seven major phases of warfare interrupted by truces of varying lengths before reaching the most dramatic moment of the war, indeed one of the most dramatic moments in all of medieval history.

Joan of Arc

How do we explain the phenomenon known as Joan of Arc? From a modern perspective we really cannot. In our age a young woman claiming to be sent by God to bring her king to victory over cruel invaders is simply a fairy tale. Yet Joan of Arc and her mission constitute historical fact. We can really comprehend Joan's role in the Hundred Years' War only by entering into the faith perspective which dominated the Middle Ages, because it was Joan's faith that made her who she was.

By 1428 the French had lost virtually every battle of the war. The pitiful young French King Charles VII controlled only a tiny region around Orleans, in central France south of Paris. France was on the verge of total collapse.

Then, suddenly, a young woman from the village of Domremy appeared: Joan, daughter of the farmer Jacques d'Arc. She told the French commander that the Archangel Michael had ordered her to come to the rescue of the king. The king's commander at first laughed at Joan but on a sudden intuition decided to seek the king's advice on the matter. Charles bade Joan to come. And as Joan—dressed now in military attire—rode to the king's court, all France learned the amazing story.

The clash in symbols produced by a young woman, assuming the masculine role of a soldier while obviously still a simple farm-girl—this tangible merging of *animus* and *anima*—so confused the French that they did not know whether to burn Joan as a witch or revere her as God's anointed messenger. While medieval Christians could tolerate the synthesis between *animus* and *anima* in their devotional life, when this synthesis became a perceptible reality, as in Joan's case, they became frightened and confused.

Charles received Joan nevertheless. Assured by French priests that she could very well be a legitimate servant of God (after the priests had had Joan's virginity verified by female inspectors), the king allowed her to assist one of his garrisons.

On the eve of battle Joan sent a message to the English commander proposing peace. When the latter rejected her offer, the French attacked with Joan fighting in the thick of battle; some 500 English soldiers were killed. Joan, now virtually deified by the French, led the French in new victories until taken captive in a battle near Compiègne (northeast France near today's Belgian frontier).

Joan's English captors summoned one of their French lackeys, Bishop Pierre Cauchon of Beauvais, and bribed him to conduct a trial in which Joan was charged with heresy. The charge was based on Joan's conviction that her "voices" were from God, and that she therefore could not submit to the authority of churchmen who ordered her to ignore the messages she had been given. Joan refused to repudiate St. Michael's command or to denounce him as a false spirit. Thus was the battle over individual versus hierarchical discernment rehearsed a century before Luther.

On May 31, 1431, Joan was burned at the stake; an English official who looked on mourned, "We have burned a saint!" The hierarchy eventually agreed with him. In 1920, perhaps thinking, "Had we lived in our forefathers' time we would not have joined them in shedding the prophets' blood" (Matthew 23:30), Pope Benedict XV canonized the Maid of Orleans a saint.

The Collapse of Order

With Joan's death—with the eradication of the Middle Ages' most tangible synthesis of *animus* and *anima*—the medieval quest for wholeness evaporated. Instead of a search for other harmony, Christian society now became dedicated to the pursuit of anarchy.

King Henry VI of England, beset by social unrest at home and eager to extract his army from his own "Vietnam," sued for peace. In 1453—the same year in which Constantinople fell to the Moslems and Gutenberg perfected his printing press by developing movable type—England retreated from France.

The Hundred Years' War had had a devastating effect on

Christian Europe. During the course of the war nearly a third of the population of Europe—perhaps as many as 25 million people—died of bubonic plague (the Black Death). Many Christians went nearly mad with grief or fear. "Flagellants" took to the streets of European cities, whipping themselves with cords as penance for sin and proclaiming the end of the world. Superstition, kept in only moderate check during times of order, became the popular religion. Astrologers, self-professed witches, fortune-tellers and nomadic prophets became for many people a new class of clergy, one supposedly possessed of the requisite power over nature to stave off the plague.

As plague and war slowly devoured agriculture by killing laborers and despoiling crops, feudalism collapsed. Knights, serfs, urban artisans and even many priests, all bereft of income—some starving to death—revolted against their social betters. In France the *Jacqueries* (peasants in France were commonly nicknamed "Jacques" by their lords) burned down manor houses and murdered and raped their previous masters. As the nobles' hired mercenaries tracked the rebels down, 20,000 were slaughtered in one month.

The war annihilated chivalry and civility. Cruelty and barbarism spread from the soldiers to the general population. Prostitution flourished as never before; a stable marriage and family were difficult to preserve.

As in previous centuries Jews served as convenient scapegoats for Christian wickedness; synagogues were burned down all over Europe. In one Parisian cemetery so many Jewish corpses awaited burial that ancient skeletons were dug up to provide space for the new arrivals. The seeds of Hitler's Germany were planted in the Middle Ages.

Could one expect that theology during this era would remain untouched by the climate of chaos, confusion and anarchy? As we saw in the last chapter, theology, too, plummeted from the state of wholeness established by Aquinas's synthesis to the depths of skepticism and the mistrust of reason signaled by William of Ockham. We can see that development reach its conclusion by investigating the fourth wave of theological discussion.

THE FOURTH WAVE OF THEOLOGICAL DISCUSSION

One would think that by the 14th century theologians would have finally reached a general consensus about the issues which had been debated since the ninth century. Wouldn't the deliberations of Radbertus, Anselm and Aquinas have produced an unchallengeable doctrinal consensus? The answer is no.

We can consider the late Middle Ages as the fourth wave of theological discussion. The first wave was the ninth century, dominated by the debates between Radbertus and Ratramnus. The second wave was the 11th century, the era of Scholasticism's origins in the writings of Anselm of Canterbury. And the third was the 13th century, the century dominated by Thomas Aquinas and his synthesis of faith and reason.

We encounter this fourth and final wave of medieval theology shortly after Thomas's death. We will notice that there were actually no new issues debated—simply new ways of debating the old issues as the struggle over the synthesis achieved by Aquinas played itself out.

Mary and the Saints

As their predecessors had done, theologians after Aquinas speculated on Mary's role and that of the saints in making Christ's salvation available to humanity. A sampling of theologians' references to Mary will give us a good idea of how Mariology had progressed from the time of Thomas Aquinas.

Thomas à Kempis (1380-1471) called Mary "Queen of Heaven, Ruler of the world,"[1] "the expiator of all the sins I have committed,"[2] "my only hope,"[3] "the total church and the total faith of the Christian church."[4] Theologians again referred to Mary as "mediatrix," in the sense that she was the means to Jesus in the same way that Jesus was the means to the Father. For example, they spoke of Mary's "maternal authority over God"[5] and "adored"[6] her as "the goddess of love, of love not impure but divine."[7]

Since Augustine had written that Mary was sinless,[8] and since he had otherwise so vociferously advanced the doctrine of original sin, it seemed logical to 14th- and 15th-century theologians to promote the doctrine of Mary's immaculate conception. Earlier theologians who had disputed this doctrine were chided. Even Bernard of Clairvaux was said to have a black mark on his soul in heaven for having questioned Mary's original sinlessness.

Bernard and Thomas Aquinas had denied the doctrine in large part because it had seemed to them to detract from Christ's redemptive power over sin—that is, how was it that Mary escaped the need for Christ's redemption? Theologians had to find some way to meet these two great saints' objections. The Franciscan theologian John Duns Scotus (1265-1308) led the way.

Scotus reasoned that Christ as perfect Redeemer had "the most perfect possible degree of mediation with respect to one creature"[9]—his mother. Scotus thus saw Christ's redemptive grace as having prevented

Mary from even contracting original sin in the first place.

For Scotus, this resolved Thomas's and Bernard's doubts since Mary could be said to have needed Christ's redemption more than anyone. Whereas other human beings needed Christ's redeeming grace to overcome original sin, Mary needed it in an even more abundant way to prevent that sin from the instant of her conception. Thus Scotus felt that the doctrine of the immaculate conception actually enhanced belief in the universal applicability of Christ's redemptive power.

The arguments of Scotus and other late-medieval Mariologists eventually prevailed in Catholic theology. On December 8, 1854, Pope Pius IX formally defined the Immaculate Conception as a doctrine canonically binding on all Catholics.

The Sacraments

John Duns Scotus was also a leader in the continuing theological effort to define the sacraments. Scotus's own definition of a sacrament, relying heavily on Augustine, was: "...a sensible sign, which by divine institution, efficaciously signifies the grace of God or the gratuitous action of God and is appointed for the salvation of a man who is still in this present life."[10]

Theologians continued to find difficulty with certain aspects of this definition. The Sacrament of Confirmation, for example, seemed unequivocally not to have been instituted by Christ but by the apostles, and Matrimony and Baptism were known before Christ's time. Further, there continued to be a multiplicity of opinions about the central sacrament—"the sacrament of each of the other sacraments"[11] as one theologian called it—the Eucharist.

The Real Presence

Since the doctrine of transubstantiation had been decisively defined by the Fourth Lateran Council (1215), only those on the fringe of orthodoxy continued pecking away at the earlier formulations of the Real Presence. Once again Augustine was used both to detract from the orthodox doctrine and to buttress it.

"Why are you preparing your teeth and your stomach? Believe, and you have already eaten." This famous rhetorical question and answer in Augustine's *Exposition on the Gospel of John*, was widely quoted to prove that the Real Presence was only a "spiritual" concept and not a "substantial" one. In response to those who cited Augustine in this way, Duns Scotus relied on the ancient argument that the Church's prayer determines its belief when he stated, "Practically all of the devotion of the Church is related to this sacrament."[12]

The three leading critics of transubstantiation—John of Paris, William of Ockham and John Wycliffe—each advanced a slightly different argument. John of Paris, a Dominican theologian (d. 1306), taught that after the consecration the substance of the bread remains as bread even though it is truly the body of Christ (very similar to Luther's later doctrine of consubstantiation). John was censured for his views and suspended from teaching.

Ockham likewise denied a change of the bread into the "substance" of Christ's body since for him this would mean that Christ was "circumscribed by place."[13] As Ockham explained his views, he seemed to be saying that God maintained the bread in its previous condition simply because otherwise one would be forced to believe something contrary to reason—namely, that the substance of the bread had actually been changed into the substance of Christ's body. Ockham thus seemed to look upon the doctrine of the Real Presence as if it were a trick God played to preserve the plausibility of what was an otherwise absurd belief.

Finally, John Wycliffe took the extreme position of denying that there was any "conversion" of bread into Christ's body whatsoever. While it was true that Christ's body was in some sense "hidden" in the bread, the bread was not transformed by "substance" into the body of Christ. For Wycliffe, the body and blood were found in the Eucharistic elements of bread and wine "figuratively" and "spiritually." Eventually Wycliffe's views evolved into the later Protestant position which looked upon the Eucharist as a mere symbol of Christ's body and blood.

As the different theological positions on the Eucharist became more inflexibly opposed to the orthodox teaching on transubstantiation, they led to the formation of entirely divergent theologies which, eventually, could only be housed in separate Churches. Thus the Eucharist, which was supposed to signify the intimate table fellowship of a common body of believers, ultimately—in the most tragic irony of the Middle Ages—came to be a principal cause of the breakup of doctrinal unity.

THE STRUGGLE TO DEFINE THE CHURCH

As the external behavior of the late-medieval Church continued to be a scandal, and as the fourth-wave theologians continued to express diverse opinions on essential doctrinal issues, the object of theological scrutiny increasingly became the Church itself. Theologians, looking out upon the war-torn landscape of Western Christendom, began to wonder if there were something fundamentally wrong not just with the *behavior* of the Church but with its very *conception.*

For the first time in the Middle Ages, *ecclesiology*—the study of the Church—became a principal concern for theologians. Opinions on the Church came from every corner—from Pope Boniface VIII who had written in his bull *Unam Sanctam* that every Christian must become subject to the pope in order to be saved to the purely spiritual definition of the Church offered by John Hus as "the totality of all who have been predestined."[14]

Pope Boniface had provided the context for the ecclesiological debate when he defined the Church as one, holy, catholic and apostolic. Theologians argued with each other vociferously as to the meaning of those words and their applicability to the concept of the Church.

Yet however theologians aligned themselves alongside Boniface's definition of Church, everyone agreed that the four "marks" of the Church—unity, holiness, catholicity, apostolicity—were unchallengeable components of the Church's constitution. These four components were the focal points around which the late medieval ecclesiological debate revolved.

The Church as One

Precisely because of the papacy's scandalous disunity during the great schism, many theologians looked elsewhere for the source of the Church's unity. It was not just "heretics" who attempted to locate that source in a council of the Church's bishops assembled together. It was not easy, however, to convince everyone to return to the early days of the Church when great decisions were made by such assemblies of bishops.

On one side stood those who could not conceive of a unified Church without one, single, visible head—the pope; on the other side stood those who argued against the physical understanding of Church altogether. Wycliffe's and Hus's argument that the Church was an entirely spiritual entity had greatly affected the basic concept of the Church. Hus could quote Augustine in appealing for a conceptualization of the Church as those who were predestined by God to salvation even if some of the elect were refused membership in the empirical, visible institution.

Cardinal Nicholas of Cusa (1401-1464) argued against the concept of a "spiritual Church of the elect." Nicholas was an ardent reformer and had worked to reconcile Hus and his followers in the Church. He realized that heresies and splinter movements could not be eradicated unless the Church entered into a true program of reform.

At first Nicholas saw the conciliar movement as the pathway to reform. But as the Council of Basle (see p. 144) became—to Nicholas's way of thinking—more and more anarchic, he became instead an advocate of papal supremacy. Nicholas criticized Hus's views on the Church. For Nicholas, unless one could posit an empirical, physical organism as the Church, one could never be certain about the existence or nature of the Church at all.

Oneness in the Church could perhaps not always be achieved in the sense that everyone acted the same way and expressed themselves uniformly. There could still be, nevertheless, a oneness based on what Nicholas of Cusa called a "varied participation in unity"[15]—that is, a oneness which, while centered on the same faith, allowed for great diversity in the expression of that faith.

The Church as Holy

The relationship between the Church's oneness and its holiness was well expressed by the French cardinal Pierre d'Ailly at the Council of Constance when he said, "There cannot be true union without reformation, nor true reformation without union."[16] This summarized the growing belief that attempts to end the papal schism were pointless without a thoroughgoing transformation of the Church from its worldly, decadent condition into a state of actual holiness.

Another French theologian, Jean Gerson (1363-1429), spoke for the reform-minded among orthodox theologians when he asked, "Has not the entire state of the Church become somehow brutal and monstrous?"[17] Even a papal official, Dietrich of Nieheim (1340-1418), after quoting Bernard of Clairvaux's characterization of the Church of the 12th century as "a den of thieves," went on to insist that since Bernard's time "the Church has gone from bad to worse."[18]

One of the leading causes of unholiness identified by theologians was the Church's great wealth. As a result, the writings of the 14th and 15th centuries sound the constant call to poverty. The lives of Christ and the apostles were continually held up as models for the clergy, especially by spiritual Franciscans such as Ubertino of Casale (d. 1341). Ubertino called the hierarchy back to the "glory of poverty" which he saw as "the foundation of the Church itself."[19] When Pope John XXII denounced such views, asserting that neither Christ nor the apostles had intended the Church to live in poverty, the pope was in turn denounced by William of Ockham and Marsilius of Padua, as we saw in the previous chapter.

In response to calls for a radical reform in the hierarchy's life-styles, Cardinal Nicholas of Cusa compared the Apostle Paul's personal confession of moral ambivalence (Romans 7:25) to the

155

Church's own highly ambivalent moral condition, concluding that moral ambivalence was simply an unpleasant fact of life. Augustine's metaphor of the Church as the net which hauled ashore both good fish and bad fish (Matthew 13:47-50) was likewise used to support the proposition that the Church's holiness did not reside in the lives of its members but in its divine institution.

The Church as Catholic

The great proponent of the Church's catholicity — its universality — was Nicholas of Cusa. His *Catholic Concordance* (1432) elaborates upon his belief that "the true Church is that which is Catholic."[20] Cusa saw the Church's catholicity as both a temporal and spatial phenomenon, for the true faith pervaded all of history as well as the boundaries of all lands.

But, if the institutional Church did indeed pervade all nations, who in that Church had the authority to define the faith?

During the height of the conciliar movement many theologians located the source of that authority in a general council. In opposition stood the first papal infallibilists who wrote such formulations as the following: "The lord pope, to whose authority it belongs to determine and declare the propositions that belong to the faith, cannot err."[21]

The late Middle Ages, with its papal schisms and conciliar fervor, was hardly the time to define a doctrine of papal infallibility. That doctrine would not come until 1870. In the meantime late medieval theologians were wary of defining the pope as the infallible spokesman for the Catholic faith. Memories of the heretical pronouncements of Pope Honorius I (see pp. 68-69) as well as of the more recent unorthodox statement by Pope John XXII that the soul does not partake of the beatific vision until after the general judgment (see p. 132) were still too fresh.

The Church as Apostolic

The difficulty in arriving at a consensus on the locus of infallibility motivated theologians to redefine the early Church's belief in its apostolic foundation. In time, apostolicity became the central focus of ecclesiological thinking.

The Apostle Paul himself had used apostolicity as a criterion for the definition of the Church: "You form a building which rises on the foundation of the apostles and prophets, with Christ Jesus himself as the capstone" (Ephesians 2:20). Jean Gerson virtually equated the Church's catholicity with its apostolicity when he wrote, "The Church is called 'catholic,' that is, universal and apostolic."[22]

Everyone spoke in favor of the Church's apostolicity but, as was the case with the other three marks of the Church, there was a wide divergence over what apostolicity meant and where it was to be found. Just as no one wanted to depart from the authority of Augustine, likewise no one wanted to be found outside the confines of apostolic teaching.

The papal schism contributed greatly to a sense of confusion and doubt about identifying the papal office with the apostolic authority to which everyone pledged support. It certainly did not help to clarify the ecclesiological discussion on apostolicity for the "apostolic see" itself to be wracked by disunity.

Yet antiquity seemed to mandate the papacy as the special repository of apostolic authority. Aside from being called the "apostolic see," the papacy was identified with "the apostolic office," and the popes' decretals were regarded as "the apostolic constitution." In contrast to this view, however, an equally ancient tradition emanating from Cyprian of Carthage (d. 258) held that all the bishops shared in the Church's apostolic order (see *The People of the Creed*, p. 112).

To resolve this discrepancy some theologians distinguished between *Petrine* primacy (which almost everyone acknowledged) and *Roman* primacy. William of Ockham, for example, argued that it was erroneous to equate "Petrine" with "Roman" since Christ had said nothing of *where* Peter's authority was to be exercised. Even an ardent advocate of papal primacy like Nicholas of Cusa reminded his readers that "if Rome were to fall, the truth of the Church would remain wherever the primacy and see of Peter would be."[23]

John Hus and his followers, on the other hand, spoke of the "primitive apostolic Church" as the only repository of apostolic authority. They defined this Church as the community of Christians who had lived until the time of Emperor Constantine the Great, or at the very latest until the era of Augustine.

Scripture Alone

As the concept of an idealized primitive Church became popular in theological circles, it was but a short step to argue that only those writings which could be infallibly traced to the hands of the apostles themselves should be considered as authoritative transmitters of the Christian faith. This, of course, would necessitate a break with all written tradition other than Scripture itself. "Scripture alone" gradually became the ever more vocal slogan of those advancing the doctrine of "primitive apostolicity."

The proponents of "Scripture alone" were unquestionably in the minority in the late Middle Ages; to advance such a view meant the overthrow of Augustine and the Fathers—the bedrock upon which the entire edifice of medieval theology had rested. Yet Wycliffe and Hus and a growing minority of other Christians were willing to base the Church's apostolic authority strictly on Scripture—apart from the Fathers, the pope and the rest of Church tradition.

In opposition to the Scripture-alone school of thought, Jean Gerson and his colleagues spoke of another basis to apostolic authority: that which "has come down to us through the successive transmission of the apostles and others, as *equivalent* to the Canonical Scripture."[24] By this "successive transmission" Gerson meant the patristic writings and that portion of Scholastic theology accepted by the Church as consistent with Scripture. Thus was laid the foundation for the Reformation's battle over Scripture and tradition.

In the end, the determination of apostolicity depended upon a choice for or against the greatest non-scriptural authority— Augustine—a choice no one would have even considered at the start of the Middle Ages. For those who remained within the Augustine consensus, however, Augustine's own words seemed to be the best answer to the Scripture-alone challenge: "For my part," the great bishop once wrote. "I should not believe the gospel except as moved by the authority of the Catholic Church."[25]

THE CULMINATION OF WESTERN SPIRITUALITY

Meister Eckhart and Speculative Mysticism

In the 14th century a new spirituality began to develop in the Low Countries and Germany. The leading spiritual writer of this movement was a German Dominican called Meister ("Master") Eckhart (1260-1327).

Eckhart, a Dominican, was naturally influenced by Thomas Aquinas and his belief in the intellect as the means of arriving at truth. Eckhart wrote that in God intellection and being are identical, by which he meant that God is pure knowledge. This greatly influenced Eckhart's spirituality, which was based on the principle that the way to attain to God as pure knowledge is through the intellect. This viewpoint represented a radical break with the traditional monastic spirituality developed by Bernard of Clairvaux, which had concentrated on the will or the "heart" as the means of attaining union with God.

Eckhart believed that the highest capacity of the soul is intellect and that the intellect is the meeting point between God's spirit and the human spirit. Eckhart defined this meeting point as "the ground of the soul," which he saw as the divine element within humanity. It is within this ground of the soul that the eternal Word transforms humanity into divinity by liberating the soul from sin.

Eckhart seemed to suggest that this process of liberation is independent of the moral and sacramental life and transcends ordinary discursive prayer. The soul is brought outside of itself, as it were, to a state of "identity" with God in true contemplation—which is a state of insensible union with the "Godhead," or God as he is in his own being, beyond all our images and ideas of him.

Critics called Eckhart's views into question. Since he had written that "God is all things, all things are God," he seemed to some a pantheist, making human beings into God through the process of divine liberation at work within the soul. But Eckhart denied that he was a pantheist:

> It is false to say that we are transformed into God....We are God's coheirs, as it is written, and that is what the *comparison* I have used means....By the grace of adoption we are united to the true son of God....To the extent that a man possesses grace and is a son of God, he has power over God, and over his works, because he wills nothing but what God wills and does.[26]

Eckhart also seemed to abolish the need for good works by making the process of the divine transformation of the human soul independent of moral action. As Eckhart wrote, "God loves souls, not exterior works."

In 1329 Pope John XXII condemned 28 of Eckhart's propositions as heretical. Eckhart died while his accusers were debating his teachings, and thus he was unable to make a response to the condemnation of a major portion of his works. Nonetheless, his influence spread in spite of the papal condemnation. His individualistic conception of the spiritual life and his disdain for good works make him a bedfellow of Wycliffe and a predecessor of Luther.

Catherine of Siena and the Anti-Speculative Reaction

Eckhart's highly speculative mysticism bothered many Christians who detected in his writings a reduction of contemplative prayer to an otherworldly Platonism beyond the grasp of ordinary Christians. As a result a reaction developed to Eckhart's speculative mysticism—a reaction in which the primacy of the intellect as a path to God was replaced by the primacy of the will.

The most famous exponent of this "affective" variety of 14th-century mysticism was Catherine of Siena (1347-1380). Catherine had experienced many visions and ecstasies from her earliest childhood.

By the age of 16, when she joined the Third Order of St. Dominic and devoted her life to serving the sick and the poor, she had already attracted a great reputation for sanctity, as well as many disciples.

In a spiritual diary entitled *Dialogue*, Catherine recorded over a period of 10 months what Christ her "Interior Master" revealed to her in prayer. The *Dialogue* is a spiritual masterpiece, but it differs entirely from the speculative treatises of the German mystics. Instead of being analytical and reasoned, it is intuitive and spontaneous.

The core of Catherine's spirituality is revealed in Christ's words to her, "Know, daughter, that I am he who is, and you are that which is not."[27] This revelation inspired in Catherine a belief in humility as the basis of spiritual life. Out of humility, she taught, we surrender ourselves completely to the needs of a neighbor as superior to all of our own desires.

ENGLISH MYSTICISM

Catherine's highly subjective and intuitive mysticism was replicated in the English school of mystical writers. English mystics such as Richard Rolle (d. 1349) wrote of contemplative prayer as a "rapture" and a "sweetness" in which God "ravishes" the soul. The greatest treatise of late-medieval English mysticism is an anonymous work entitled *The Cloud of Unknowing*. At odds with Eckhart, it believes God may be experienced only in love (through the will) and not by knowledge (through the intellect).

The author of *The Cloud* describes contemplation as a penetration by love through "a cloud of unknowing" in which God is hidden. One moves through this cloud only through "stirrings of love." *The Cloud* is unique in that the author describes an actual technique to dispose one toward contemplative union. The technique consists in the passive repetition of a short word—such as *Jesus, love, Abba* or the like—epitomizing one's desire to surrender to God's gift of contemplation.

English mysticism culminated in the *Revelations of Divine Love* of Julian of Norwich (1342-1413). Like Catherine of Siena, Julian was a female mystic with a profoundly intuitive and subjective vision. In a series of 16 revelations she was granted extraordinary experiences of Christ's passion and of the inner dynamics of the Trinity. Her revelations led Julian to conclude that God's love is the solution to all problems and evils.

Julian sums up her contemplative experience by saying, "Would you understand your Lord's meaning? Understand it well: Love was his meaning. Who showed it to you? Love. What did he show you? Love. Why did he show it to you? For love."[28]

The *Devotio Moderna*

The movement toward a subjective spirituality similar to that taught by Catherine of Siena and the English mystics came to full flower in a movement originating in Holland known as the *devotio moderna*, or "modern devotion."

The founder of this movement was a layman, Gerard Groote. About 1374 Gerard was converted from a life of ease and indulgence to one of evangelical poverty. After spending three years in a monastery, he became a traveling preacher in Holland, in the tradition of the mendicant life-style popular a century earlier. A strong critic of clerical abuses, he was censured in 1383. After first helping to organize a community of women inspired by his ideals, Groote associated himself with a like-minded group of men who became known as the Brethren of the Common Life.

The Brethren took no vows and continued whatever careers or livelihoods they had been engaged in before joining the community. Priests as well as laymen joined the fraternity, although the life-style remained conspicuously unclerical by its simplicity and poverty. The Brethren founded many schools for poor children in both Holland and Germany.

Groote's spirituality was entirely this-worldly. Suspicious of Eckhart's speculative mysticism, Groote and the Brethren defined spirituality entirely in terms of inner conversion, repentance and apostolic service. The only technique of contemplation which Groote and his followers trusted was "the imitation of the manhood of Christ."

One member of the Brethren, Thomas à Kempis (see p. 151), wrote a biography of Gerard Groote as well as a treatise summarizing the Brethren's spirituality. The latter work—*The Imitation of Christ*—became one of the most widely read books of all time. In it Thomas summarized his negative views on speculative mysticism and thus showed the entirely practical orientation of the *devotio moderna*: "Of what use is it to discourse loftily on the Trinity if you lack humility and hence displease the Trinity? Truly, lofty words do not make one holy and righteous, but a virtuous life makes one dear to God."[29]

Instead of the path of speculative mysticism, Thomas pointed his readers toward the path of penance and service. His spirituality is based upon meditation on Christ's humanity as a means to the awareness of his divinity.

He characterizes contemplation as a "sideways look" at God—as a small taste of the beatific vision which can be enjoyed only in heaven. "Our first effort," Thomas wrote, "should be to become absorbed into the life of Jesus."[30] By this Thomas meant not simply leading an exemplary life of virtue, but being transformed from within into the consciousness of Jesus through meditation on Jesus' humanity.

The difference between Thomas à Kempis and Meister Eckhart is not the difference between action and contemplation. Both writers defined a mystical spirituality in which contemplation plays an essential part.

The critical issue is the degree to which each manifests incarnational thinking. Thomas and the *devotio moderna* conceived of the spiritual life as an incarnational relationship with the universal Christ of history at every level of one's being. Eckhart and the speculative tradition tended toward a nonincarnational experience beyond the senses—very similar to the Byzantine mystagogy advanced by such writers as Pseudo-Dionysius and Maximus the Confessor (see p. 21).

As the advocates of the *devotio moderna* gained increasing influence, they effectively brought an end to speculative mysticism and with it Scholasticism's speculative analysis of great theological issues. Subjective feeling and the personal experience of Christ within one's heart became the touchstone of late medieval spirituality.

The *devotio moderna* thus signaled the end of Aquinas's great synthesis between faith and reason. Henceforth, in many quarters, faith sought to leave reason behind and to express itself solely through subjective experience. Martin Luther would soon write, "Reason is the greatest enemy that faith has....She is the Devil's greatest whore."[31]

Ironically, that Catholic faith which had so brilliantly and passionately provided an answer to the medieval Christian's quest for wholeness would shortly become simply what each person subjectively experienced. Only a half-century after the death of Thomas à Kempis, Martin Luther would insist that each Christian stood alone as the sole arbiter of the faith. As that view gained popularity, whatever wholeness medieval Christians had achieved splintered into a thousand pieces, and the "People of the Faith" became the "People of Anguish."

CONCLUSION

A Mixed Achievement

By now we realize that the medieval Church's achievement is a mixed one. How shall we sort out the bad from the good? Let's speak once again of events, thought and faith. At the end of the Middle Ages these three elements of the Church's personality—its behavior, theology and spirituality—have yet to be integrated into a working whole.

ON THE EVE OF THE REFORMATION: THE CHURCH IN DISARRAY

In its behavior the Church is still an insecure young man, frightened by the aggressive posturing of the other insecure males of its day, and frightened too by its attraction to the feminine energy which so captivates its attention. As a result, the Church asserts itself through boasting, bullying and violence. It fears to make itself vulnerable, to allow itself to become receptive; it feels instead that it must dominate and control. Above everything else, the Church in its behavioral aspect seeks control, order and certainty. By seeking these it hopes to dominate the changing forces which frighten it.

The Church's spirituality, on the other hand, exhibits precisely the opposite tendencies: receptivity, openness, patience and love. While in its behavior the Church is masculine, in its faith it has become overwhelmingly feminine. It has adopted the role of Mary rather than that of Martha; it realizes it is called not to control and manipulate others, but to wait on the Lord and receive from him what he has to say, in order to follow *his* lead rather than to dwell on its own compulsive busy-ness.

Yet the feminine tendency to define faith in terms of contemplative experience has not yielded completely positive results either. In its desire for the experiential taste of union with its Lord, the Church is in danger of neglecting the challenges of its environment. Living the *anima* to the exclusion of the *animus* means virtually living in a state of nondescript passivity. This easygoing vacuousness does not lead the Church to holistic growth any more than does flexing its muscles and competing macho-like with its rivals. What the Church needs at this point is to integrate and harmonize the two poles of its personality—the masculine energy put into play by its behavior, and the feminine energy set in motion by its faith.

The bond which serves to link these two extremes together is the Church's intellectual life—theology. This aspect of the Church's personality seems confused at the end of the Middle Ages. Just as the synthesis of faith and reason was worked out by the Scholastics, along came a fourth wave of Christian thinking which threw theology into chaos. Now no one is sure what to think. Theology is tugged at from two directions—represented by the Church's masculine behavior and its feminine spirituality.

In which direction will theology go? Or will it go in neither direction? Will it stand and harden, torn between two opposites, locked in place by indecision? Theology seems timid and uncertain. It acts as if it were awaiting some fateful push from a mind that will once again make clear-cut judgments about the truths of revelation.

On the eve of the Reformation, then, we find the Church living not in a state of wholeness—the goal that it had struggled so hard to achieve—but in a state of disharmony and confusion. The Church is disoriented and perplexed; it knows that order and discipline are essential, but it has learned that brutality often results when it imposes order and discipline out of fear and insecurity.

The Church wants to bring to the surface—to the level of its behavior—its sense of faith as contemplative relationship with the Lord. It wants that portion of itself which sees the world from the eyes of the threatened and insecure young male to accept that aspect of its personality which sees the world from the feminine perspective of openness, patience and docility. Yet the bridge between these two impulses—the Church's mind—is clouded by turmoil. In one sense, then, we leave the Middle Ages in a state of incompletion and irresolution.

Achievements of Medieval Christianity

At the same time, however, we must acknowledge that the Church of the Middle Ages has made remarkable and lasting achievements. In terms of behavior it has courageously resisted many threats to its independence. It has survived its difficult adolescence in one piece. This is no small feat when one considers where it started—in a world dominated by the fractious breakup of Roman imperial unity. No matter how much we may dislike the means the Church has used at times to preserve its self-identity, we can say without compromise that the very idea of a Christian society and, indeed, the very preservation of Christianity owe their existence to the unifying forces of medieval Roman Catholicism and Byzantine orthodoxy.

In terms of the Church's thought, we can likewise look upon the Christian Middle Ages as a time of positive growth. Never before and never since has there appeared an intellectual achievement to match that of the Middle Ages. In no other time have the intellectual forces of an entire age come as close as in the Middle Ages to establishing a unified theory to explain God, the world and humanity's relationship to God and the world.

Finally, in terms of faith, the achievement of the Middle Ages in developing contemplative spirituality is something which our own century sorely needs to recapture. For many people today, life is merely the senses, and happiness entirely sensual gratification. As a result, our age is permeated by a crude materialism which has desiccated and threatens to destroy the human spirit. By contrast, the Christian Middle Ages, through defining faith as contemplative experience, constantly held up before society the transcendent dimension of life and gave Christians a taste of the joy which only a spiritually focused life can bring.

SYMBOLS OF AN ERA: INNOCENT, THOMAS, BERNARD

If I had to pick three people who personify the best of the three characteristics we have just discussed, I would choose Pope Innocent III, Thomas Aquinas and Bernard of Clairvaux.

Innocent established order and stability in a Church made up of a growing and diverse population. Innocent—as our personification of the Church's behavior—imposed order and stability not for their own sakes, but to establish the essential cohesiveness which any earthly community needs to function.

In doing so he tried to act out of love and with a sense of respect for the worth of others. He could dominate without being domineering, be assertive without being aggressive and lead without doing violence to the human spirit. Innocent, as well as any mortal could, made the universal Church an incarnate reality, a community of sinners struggling to be saints, but a community nonetheless. With Innocent the Church achieved a degree of commonality not seen since.

Thomas Aquinas—our personification of Christian thought—raised theology to a plateau from which the human mind could make a rationally satisfying evaluation of the ways of God among human beings. More than anyone in history, Thomas united in his writings the impulses to believe and to know. He appreciated better than anyone in his day the wonder of a God who created the human will with its need for believing and the human mind with its thirst for understanding. With Thomas—if only for a brief moment—Christians could know and believe in complete accord.

With Thomas, heart and intellect were brought into a state of harmony as they worked together to make the gospel a real event in a real world. Christians today unfortunately have little use for Thomas's synthesis. The extremes of modern Christianity either suppress the intellect by turning faith into narcissistic emotionalism, or do violence to the heart by proclaiming a purely cognitive gospel that never escapes from seminaries and universities.

Finally, in Bernard of Clairvaux, the personification of medieval Christian faith, the Church achieved the height of contemplative spirituality. Bernard harnessed the mystical energies of Augustine and earlier giants of the spiritual life and made those energies available to Dominic, Francis, Catherine and all those in the Middle Ages who sought to come to wholeness through the Spirit's embrace of mystical love. Bernard rises above the Middle Ages as a sort of universal spiritual Father for all time, directing all who yearn for the taste and touch of the interior life.

Perhaps we should more accurately characterize Bernard as the universal spiritual "Father/Mother." Bernard, who had integrated within himself the tendencies of both *animus* and *anima*, brought Christian faith into a state of wholeness—a state in which the masculine and the feminine in human experience are harmonized before a God who is neither male nor female, but the supreme and eternal symphony of *animus* and *anima*. The glory of the Christian Middle Ages and their most significant achievement was this elaboration of the contemplative dimension of Christian faith.

Innocent, Thomas and Bernard—symbols of the three different channels by which the Christian experience was passed on to future centuries. The Christian experience coursed in each channel in a different way: In its behavior medieval Christianity expressed itself in the establishment of the Church as a universal community; in its theology medieval Christianity brought reason and revelation into harmony; in its faith medieval Christianity developed the deep resources of the human spirit. Together the three channels of medieval Christianity constituted a remarkable degree of wholeness, an achievement never since matched and a goal which humanity still seeks.

NOTES

Chapter One

1. Maximus the Confessor, "Epistles," 13 (2:8).*
2. *Ibid.,* "Scholia on the Ecclesiastical Hierarchy," 5, 3 (2:12).
3. *Ibid.*
4. *Ibid.,* "400 Chapters on Charity," 3.99 (2:33; emphasis added).
5. Isidore of Seville, "Sentences," 2, I.5 (3:20).
6. Boniface, "Sermons," 8.1 (3:24).
7. Bede, "Homilies," 1.7 (3:29).
8. Alcuin, "Epistles," 89 (3:29).
9. Bede, "History of the Church," 5.12 (3:33).
10. *Ibid.,* "Exposition of 1 Peter" (3:45).
11. Aldhelm, "Hymns," 1.6, 4.1.2 (3:46).
12. Isidore of Seville, "Origins," 7.12.13 (3:48).
13. Hincmar of Reims, "On the Rights of Metropolitans," 18 (3:48).

Chapter Two

1. Charlemagne, "Epistles of Alcuin," 93, 137ff., *History of the Church,* Hubert Jedin, ed., 10 vols. (The Crossroad Publishing Co., 1982; 3:89).
2. Methodius, "Synodicon," (2:145).

Chapter Three

1. Hincmar of Reims, "On Predestination," 31 (2:51).
2. John Scotus Erigena, "On Predestination," 1.4 (2:51).
3. Florus of Lyons, "On Holding Immovably to the Truth of Scripture," 1 (2:51).
4. Alcuin, "Against Felix," 1.11 (2:58).
5. Hincmar of Reims, "On the Deity as One and Not Three," 9 (2:58).
6. Gottschalk, "A Slip of Paper" (2:60).
7. Hincmar of Reims, "On the Deity as One and Not Three," 9 (2:60).
8. *Ibid.,* 10 (2:62).
9. Gottschalk, "Responses," 7 (2:85).
10. Hincmar of Reims, "On Predestination," 27 (2:91).
11. Radbertus, "On the Body and Blood of the Lord," 1.11 (2:76).
12. Ratramnus, "On the Body and Blood of the Lord," 57 (2:77; emphasis added).

---

* Unless otherwise indicated, the numbers in parentheses after a quoted source refer to volume and page numbers of Jaroslav Pelikan's *The Christian Tradition,* 4 vols. (University of Chicago Press, 1974).

13. Radbertus, "On the Body and Blood of the Lord," 8 (2:79; emphasis added).
14. John Scotus Erigena, "On Natures," 1.13 (2:105).
15. *Ibid.*, 5.4 (2:95).
16. *Ibid.*, 1.72 (2:102).
17. John Scotus Erigena, "Expositions of the Celestial Hierarchies," 15.5 (2:104).
18. Florus of Lyons, "Against Erigena," pr. (2:98).
19. Ildefonsus of Toledo, "The Virginity of Mary," 12 (2:69).
20. Ambrose Autpert, "On the Feast of the Assumption," 11 (2:70).
21. Radbertus, "On the Parturition of Mary," 1.16 (2:71).
22. Ambrose Autpert, *op. cit.*, 3 (2:72).

Chapter Five

1. Pope Leo II, "Epistles," 3 (2:152).
2. Nicetas Stethatos, "Antidialogue," 15.1 (2:175).
3. Pseudo-Photius, "Against the Franks," 8 (2:176).
4. John of Antioch, "Treatise on the Azymes," 2 (2:177).
5. Michael Cerularius, "Epistles to Peter of Antioch," 1.2 (2:177).
6. Humbert, "Response to the Book of Nicetas Stethatos," 11 (2:178).
7. Michael Cerularius, *op. cit.*, 1.14 (2:181).
8. *Ibid.*, 1.12 (2:185).
9. Peter of Antioch, "Epistle to Michael Cerularius," 11 (2:185).
10. Gregory the Great, "Homilies on the Gospels," 2.26.2 (2:193).
11. Augustine, "On the Trinity," 5.11.12 (2:196).

Chapter Six

1. Rupert of Deutz, "On Divine Offices," 6.2 (3:142).
2. Baldwin of Ford, "Tractates," 7 (3:162).
3. *Ibid.*, (3:166).
4. Peter Damian, "Hymns," B. 38.2 (3:168).
5. Bernard of Clairvaux, "Advent Sermons," 2.5 (3:168).
6. *Ibid.*, "On All Saints' Day," 5.5 (3:175).
7. Odo of Cluny, "Life of St. Gerald," 4.9 (3:182).
8. Guibert of Nogent, "On the Relics of the Saints," 1.2 (3:183).
9. Baldwin of Ford, "The Sacrament of the Altar," 2.1.3 (3:203).
10. Fourth Lateran Council (3:203-204).
11. Alger of Liege, "On the Sacraments," 1.8 (3:206).
12. Pope Alexander III, "The Sentences of Roland" (3:207).
13. Guigo II, "Scale of Paradise," *A History of Christian Spirituality*, Louis Bouyer, 3 vols. (The Seabury Press, 1982; 1:159).
14. Odo of Cluny, *op. cit.*, 2.16 (3:126).
15. Bouyer (2:195).

Chapter Seven

1. Gerhoh of Reichersberg, "On the Edification of God" (Bouyer, 2:257).
2. Stephen of Muret, "Sermon" (*Ibid.*, 2:258).
3. Jacques de Vitry, "Two Books" (*Ibid.*).
4. Albert of Magdeburg (Jedin, 4:212).

Chapter Eight

1. Alexander of Hales, "Summa Theologica," 1, q. 1, cap. 1, *A History of Christian Thought*, Justo Gonzalez, 3 vols. (Abingdon Press, 1971; 2:247).
2. Thomas Aquinas, "Summa Theologica," I, q. 2, art. 2 (*Ibid.*, 2:260).
3. *Ibid.*, I, I, 8 (3:285).
4. Bernard of Clairvaux, "Sermons on the Song of Songs," 3.1.1 (3:304).
5. Richard of St. Victor, "On the Erudition of the Inner Man," I. 2, 2.10 (3:304).
6. Bonaventure, "The Journey of the Mind to God," 3.1 (3:305).
7. *Ibid.*, 4.6.
8. *Ibid.*, 1.7.
9. *Ibid.*, 4.4.
10. *Ibid.*, 7.3.

Chapter Nine

1. William of Malmesbury, "Life of St. Wulfstan," *Popular Religion in the Middle Ages*, R. and C. Brooke (Thames and Hudson, 1984; 105).
2. *Ibid.*, 146.
3. Orderic Vitalis, "Ecclesiastical History" (*Ibid.*, 148).
4. Master Herman, "Epitome of Theology" (3:212).
5. "Life of Christina Markyate" (Brooke, 112).
6. Wolfram von Eschenbach, "Parzival" (*Ibid.*, 115).

Chapter Ten

1. William of Ockham, "Brief Statement on the Tyrannical Principate," II, 4 (Jedin, IV:366).
2. Marsilius of Padua, "Defender of the Peace," II, 2, 3 (*Ibid.*, 362).
3. Acts of the Council of Constance, *"Haec Sancta,"* Ibid , 448ff.
4. *Ibid.*, 463.

Chapter Eleven

1. Thomas à Kempis, "Sermons on the Life and Passion of Our Lord," 6 (4:39).
2. *Ibid.*, "Prayers and Meditations on the Life of Christ," 1.2.26 (4:40).
3. *Ibid.*, "Prayers," 7.

4. *Ibid.*, "Prayers and Meditations on the Life of Christ," 1.2.26.
5. Jean Gerson, "On the Spiritual Life of the Soul," 3 (4:41).
6. *Ibid.*, "Commentary on the Magnificat," 11.
7. *Ibid.*, "Sermons," 230, 215, 248 (4:42).
8. Augustine, "Nature and Grace," 36.42 (4:45).
9. John Duns Scotus, "Question Whether the Blessed Virgin Was Conceived in Original Sin" (4:47).
10. *Ibid.*, "Oxford Commentary on the Sentences" (4:50-51).
11. Nicholas of Cusa, "Epistles," 2 (4:52).
12. John Duns Scotus, "Oxford Commentary on the Sentences," 4.8.1.3 (4:55).
13. William of Ockham, "On the Sacrament of the Altar," 3 (4:57).
14. John Hus, "On the Church," 1.B (4:69).
15. Nicholas of Cusa, *op. cit.*, 1 (4:79).
16. Pierre D'Ailly, "Sermons," 2 (4:85).
17. Jean Gerson, "Sermons," 212 (4:86).
18. Dietrich of Nieheim, "Invective Against Pope John XXII," 14 (4:86-87).
19. Ubertino of Casale, "The Tree of the Crucified Life of Jesus," 3.9 (4:88).
20. Nicholas of Cusa, "Catholic Concordance," 1.12 (4:99).
21. Guido Terrena, "On the Infallible Magisterium of the Roman Pontiff" (4:107).
22. Jean Gerson, "Against Pedro de Luna," 1.8 (4:110).
23. Nicholas of Cusa, "Epistles," 2 (4:117).
24. Jean Gerson, "On the Spiritual Life of the Soul," 2 (4:121; emphasis added).
25. Augustine, "Against the Epistle of Manicheus," 5 (4:125).
26. Meister Eckhart (Bouyer, 2:387; emphasis added).
27. Catherine of Siena, "Dialogue" (*Ibid.*, 2:412).
28. Julian of Norwich, "Revelations of Divine Love" (*Ibid.*, 2:426).
29. Thomas à Kempis, "The Imitation of Christ," I, 1, 7ff.
30. *Ibid.*, I, 1, 3.
31. "Luther's Works," VI, 142-148, *The Reformation*, Will Durant (Simon and Schuster, 1957; 370).

INDEX